What to Do When the
BLESSINGS STOP

When God Sends Famine

What to Do When the
BLESSINGS STOP

When God Sends Famine

© 2002 Virginia Hull Welch

ISBN - 978-0-9888739-4-0
E-Book ISBN - 978-0-9888739-5-7

What to Do When the Blessings Stop –
When God Sends Famine

All scripture references are taken from the King James
Version unless otherwise noted.

Published by Virginia Hull Welch, 2013
www.ginnywelch.com

Cover design by Reynaldo Licayan

If I shut up heaven that there be no rain, or if I command the locusts to devour the land, or if I send pestilence among my people;

If my people, which are called by my name, shall humble themselves, and pray, and seek my face, and turn from their wicked ways; then will I hear from heaven, and will forgive their sin, and will heal their land. II Chron. 7:13–14

Contents

Other by Books by Virginia Hull Welch

The Lesson
Romantic Comedy Based on a True Story

Crazy Woman Creek
Inspirational Western Fiction

The Hiss from Hell Only Women Hear:
Is It Truth or Is It Tradition? (2013)

*To my children: Juliet, John Carl, and Emerald,
may you always walk in truth, and in loving memory of
Greg*

The Wake-Up Call

Years have passed, yet the memory of that dreadful day still surfaces from time to time, usually when I am alone. With an aching that time has helped diminish, I recount silently to myself in a dark and chilly corner of my soul the day I called out to God in the face of looming tragedy, but He refused to hear.

It hadn't always been that way. Prior to 1991 I was accustomed to having my prayers answered; God blessed my family. My husband had a rewarding job he loved with the federal government, and I was working as an editor at a prestigious Alabama publishing house. We had two healthy young children, a girl and a boy, and lived in a fine home in a nice neighborhood. We tithed, gave offerings, and earned enough money to stay in the black. The only debts we had were our mortgage and low-interest college loans, which we were paying down monthly. We regularly attended an active, growing Christian church and entertained Christians and non-Christians in our home.

Life was good, and so I expected that with my husband's upcoming transfer to Washington, D.C. God would bless us more: a good church, a better job for me, and an even nicer home for all of us.

But everything, and I mean everything, went horribly wrong. When the government's transfer agent made us an offer on our Alabama home, we were stunned to see that it was below the amount of our mortgage. We certainly couldn't accept an offer that would leave us in debt for a home we no longer owned, so we tried to sell it through a real estate agent without the government's help. We tried and tried to sell our beautiful, well-maintained house, but even when we lowered the price to just cover the mortgage it still didn't sell. Time passed and we couldn't delay our move any longer, so with our two children and a new baby, we left Alabama, found a rental house in northern Virginia, and continued to try to make payments on both properties. We couldn't keep that up very long, though, because overnight we went from two incomes and one house payment to one income and two house payments. For the first time in our lives we began to fall behind on our mortgage payment. Finally the deadline to make all back payments on the Alabama house came and went, and though I cried wildly to God to send us a buyer, He did not deliver us. We lost our house.

Yet strangely, the day after it foreclosed, our real estate agent received seven offers from buyers who didn't know about the foreclosure. One offer was for our full asking price. I was jolted by this revelation, though I had no idea what it meant. I strongly suspected that the offers had been divinely held back.

Before that awful day arrived, there were other, less shocking but similarly disturbing attacks on our finances. After leaving behind in Alabama the most desirable and satisfying job I'd ever had to follow my husband to his new assignment, I, who had never had any problem getting a job in my field, couldn't find a job no matter how hard I tried. My period of unemployment lasted for months. Months stretched into years, which of course only contributed to our depressing financial troubles.

Then about the same time as the sky was falling over our Alabama home, my husband's employer informed him that they had errantly overpaid us thousands of dollars in travel expenses, and they wanted their money, now, and we didn't have it. Then the IRS contacted us, and for the first time in years we owed them money, several thousand dollars, and of course, we didn't have that either. Then there was the car accident in our newly purchased family van and a repair bill for several thousand. The portion we owed, per the insurance company, went into the hundreds. It might as well have been in the millions. We didn't have it.

So went our lives for several years. The bad news was so unrelenting that there were days when I'd wake up and the first thought that came to mind was, "I wonder what awful news I'll get today?" Finally, and on top of everything else, annoyed over some petty offense, we left our local fellowship and began looking for another church. Unwittingly we cut ourselves off from our single source of encouragement in a town where we had no family and because we were relatively new to the area, few friends.

What is going on? I didn't know, but whatever it was, I did know it was spiritual. Nothing, absolutely nothing we did prospered as before. For me it was never the question, "Where is God?" I knew where He was: right in the middle of this. The question for me was, *why is God not answering our prayers?* The fact that He wasn't answering was, to me, his real message, a rebuke so loud it kept me up at night, fearful of what might be behind his evident displeasure. I sensed that God had turned his back and shut his ears, while we struggled on alone, feeling abandoned, losing nearly everything. Our church, our house, our good credit rating, my job, our peace—all gone. Mercifully I did not lose my marriage or family, but throughout the ordeal there were times I thought I would lose my mind.

That's because I used to think that if I just prayed hard enough, fasted long enough, confessed the right scriptures, walked in mountain-moving faith, that if I did all the right spiritual exercises, I could make all the bad stuff go away. Well, I was half right. Faith can move a mountain.

But what we faced was not a mountain. It was famine. This is the word God spoke into my spirit one day in the midst of the confusion. I had never heard teaching on the subject, yet I knew intuitively that what we were experiencing was exactly that and that it was from God. I had read many times the biblical accounts of famine, but of course, they were always in the Bible, stories from the past about dead people. I had not met a single living Christian who had experienced anything like I was experiencing. But the word in my spirit was so certain, and our circumstances so famine-like, that I knew that God had given me a revelation to bank on. He had given me light to guide me through the very real, very dark cloud of death that hung over our home.

God still sends famine. But what He sends now is different from the drought and pestilence you read about in the Old Testament. And don't confuse famine like my family experienced with the mere annoying roadblocks Satan throws in your path to detour you on your Christian journey. Famine is different. You can't move it out of the road by blasting away at it with your faith. You can't move it by the slow, methodical dump truck method either, hauling it away load by load through daily positive confession. The famine God sends is, by his design, a long, thorough ordeal meant to get your attention, to force you to examine yourself, to make deep and lasting changes in your soul. And when He's done with you, He alone will remove the famine and restore what you have lost. He restores you and what's yours because He loves you. He sends famine for the same reason.

Of course, years ago I knew nothing of these truths. I knew only that God wasn't answering our prayers and that something was very, very wrong.

1. Recognize the Signs of Famine

How do you counsel the Christian who never succeeds? Who never achieves his or her timely business plans, even with judicious planning and hard work? Who is unemployed for months and months though the church prays and prays? Who loses home, business, family? Do you tell this person to pray more? Study the Bible more? Keep up the positive confession? Is God angry? Or is He just saying "no" to the anguished pleadings of this unhappy soul? What hope do you offer?

Or is this person you? Do you feel that nothing you do prospers? That all you do is scrape by? Is your life just one disappointment after another? How do you explain the loss and pain that result when your prayer goes unanswered in your deepest hour of need? Are you secretly tempted, even briefly, to believe that things will never get better? Are you ashamed of the dark, hopeless thoughts that assail you, thoughts no Christian should ever think?

1

Do you look back and remember a time in your life, unlike now, when the blessings of God—on your relationships, your job or ministry, your body, your wallet—were a daily experience? Do you spend hours agonizing over what awful thing you could have done to bring about so much disaster in your life? (Or perhaps you know…) Have you experienced so many calamities and setbacks that it seems as if an unseen force is arrayed against you, opposing you at every turn in your efforts to succeed at nearly everything?

Your assessment of your life may be right on target. There may be an unseen force opposing you, a spiritual one, standing in the way of your success. But this force is not the horned type with a pitchfork. Nor is he an enemy to bind and resist with spiritual weapons. In fact, this force may not be an enemy at all.

The force that opposes you may be God. Your grievous circumstances could be the result of famine, a spiritual experience God sends to correct his people. I know now that God sent famine into our lives and I know why He sent it. But I won't share the reason with you because frankly, you don't need to know. What you need to know is why God has sent famine to *you*, and you need to know what to do to have God remove it.

Because we have been, by and large, taught more about God's grace, love, and forgiveness than we have about his judgment, we do not carry a mental picture of a God who opposes his people. We've been taught that God is for us, not against us, that He'll forgive us 70x7 times if we confess our sins. The mental picture we cling to is of a gentle Jesus, clothed in a white robe, serene and smiling, surrounded by little children. This image of God lines up with his word, yet there is more to know about God.

God never changes. He is the same yesterday, today, and forever. That's why Old Testament stories are just as useful for studying his nature as stories about Jesus in the New. The revelation we have of Him from the Old Testament does not contradict the New. It enhances it. God recorded his dealings with his people in the Old and New Testaments because He wants us to use them for instruction in life now. He recorded their failures to spare us their suffering; He recorded their successes to inspire us to righteousness. So to understand God's dealings with us now, we must study how He dealt with them then.

Just as God does not change, human nature does not change. Individuals change from year to year, even day to day, but generation to generation human nature does not change. The adamic nature passes from one generation to the next and each suffers its bondage until they find Christ. In this regard, no one changes. The same weaknesses of the flesh, to one degree or another, appear in every generation. Jeremiah 17:9 says the heart of man is desperately wicked. That was true of people then, it is true of people now. Galatians 5 lists the many sins of the flesh. These sins were evident in the population then; they are evident in the world now.

God never tolerates sin. Repeatedly in the Old Testament God used an effective method to awaken his people from spiritual sloth and pressure them to repent: He cut off their food supply until they were so hungry they cried to Him for mercy. The Bible calls this experience "famine." His method worked because our hearts are intimately bound to our natural source of supply, be it jobs, businesses, farms, or whatever. We

3

need to eat. When God threatens what is dear to us, He has our attention.

That's why God says in Ezekiel 14:13 that He uses famine as an attention-getter.

When the land sinneth against me by trespassing grievously, then will I stretch out mine hand upon it, and will break the staff of the bread thereof, and will send famine upon it.

God still sends famine to his disobedient people, because like the Jews of old, we too are pressured by lack and motivated by plenty. It is our nature. Though it is true that, unlike the Jews we are under grace and redeemed from the curses of the law by the redemptive work of Christ, and though it is true that in Christ we are spiritually complete, it is also true that now as then God's blessings are conditional. We must put Him first and obey his word. If we fail to do either God will discipline us. He disciplines us, his children, in love under a covenant of grace. But speaking from experience, it *feels* like judgment.

By famine I don't mean necessarily years of drought and no crops, though it could be expressed that way. *Famine* is from Hebrew *ra'ab*, which means hunger, dearth, or famished. In the Bible, famine is sometimes translated from another Hebrew word, *kaphan*, which means hunger, too. But *kaphan* paints a distinctly painful picture, depicting one who is stooped with emptiness and pain. No better word exists to describe the Christian who has suffered a long period of financial lack, failure in life in general, and the frustration and disappointment of unanswered prayer,

4

especially when a critical deadline passes and you are left without the heavenly help you cry for.

By prosper I don't mean only to do well financially. To prosper means exactly what it says in the *American Heritage Dictionary*: "To be fortunate or successful, especially in terms of one's finances, to thrive." When the life of Christ flows through you, your endeavors are marked by what the world calls good fortune or success. When the life of Christ flows into any area of your life, that area thrives. Though all Christians face disappointments and faith tests, *over the long haul* the person who lives by faith, hooked up and yielded to the source of life, can believe God for and learn how to walk in good health, a happy and satisfying marriage, blessings in business, friendship, promotion in career or ministry, and a gradual enlargement and strengthening of all that is important. You thrive because that is what Christ promised in John 10:10: an abundant, overcoming life now in addition to life after death.

It is difficult to be an overcomer and to teach others to be so when you're worried about where the rent money will come from; that's why prosperity includes but is not limited to your wallet. (A word about prosperity: This is not a money book and it's certainly not a book about getting rich. This IS a book about throwing off the spiritual curse of chronic lack and failure—famine—that can, and in most cases, does affect your finances. The amount of money you need to feel comfortable is entirely between you and God; I will not touch upon it here. Suffice it to say, whatever amount you call "enough," a lot or a little, Satan is conspiring to rob you of it—likely he's already done so and that's why you picked up this book. So keep reading.)

Famine hurts your finances, however, because we don't deal in corn and pigs any more, and the few that do still measure their prosperity in terms of money. No matter how prosperous a modern farmer is, he still has to convert his sows to sawbucks in order to buy shirts and socks at Sears. If you're an opera singer and lose your voice, you may think what you have is a health problem, but in reality you could be on the cusp of a financial famine. The same is true if you're an evangelist and someone lies about your character. When speaking engagements fall off, you may interpret that as a persecution problem, but famine could be just around the corner. If you make custom leather shoes and animal rights activists picket your store, even your best customers may be intimidated and go elsewhere. That doesn't seem like famine, does it? But with famine nowadays it always comes down to finances, and if you've lived a while, you know that when your finances fall apart your whole life hurts.

Why do we assume that now, in New Testament times, famine is no longer a tool God uses to correct his children? We seem to think that because we have no fields to suffer drought we are beyond the reach of famine. But because we changed from a mostly agrarian society to a mostly technological one, did God change? Has human nature changed? True, we have the Holy Spirit now, and we have been given a new, divine nature. But do we consistently walk in our new nature? Do we never need correction? Is anyone totally free from the tendency to carnality and pride? Ideally we should be corrected by the word and the Spirit alone, but even the most sanctified miss it from time to time.

III John 1:2 tells us that God desires you to prosper and be in health in the same way that your soul (inner man) prospers and is healthy:

Beloved, I wish above all things that thou mayest prosper and be in health, even as thy soul prospereth.

Your soul prospers as you feed on God's word. Are you reading and meditating on it regularly? If you don't voluntarily renew your mind through the word and attend to spiritual things first, to cause your spirit to prosper, then God has no choice but to discipline you through the natural realm, because that's where we put our attention when we take it off the spiritual. (Where else can we put it? In God there is no third dimension. We either have our minds on the natural or spiritual world.) He does this by removing his blessings, which thwarts our efforts to prosper in the natural realm. This is famine.

Even when we recognize the signs of famine in our lives, we tend to blame our troubles on Satan. But Satan is always under God's thumb. He is just God's errand boy. On what date in history was Satan promoted to a role of greater autonomy? We give the little pipsqueak too much credit. Satan may work the famine into our circumstances, but he does so only at God's command. Elisha told the Shunammite woman in II Kings 8 that the Lord Himself had commanded a famine upon the land. Other verses in the Bible, which we will soon review, read similarly. We never read that Satan called for a famine. So binding him isn't going to do you any good when God is using him to do the dirty work in the first place.

This is not to say that every downturn in your life is evidence of a divinely-sent famine. Satan has a pernicious track record of opposing the most upright of saints because he attacks everyone who desires to serve God. It's part of our sanctifying process. By examining the famines of the Bible, I hope to help you determine whether what you're experiencing is a God-ordained famine designed to bring you to repentance, or just another bothersome arrow designed to penetrate your shield of faith. Understanding the difference will make your responses smarter and maybe even shorten your ordeal.

The entire world is fallen. Just as the unseen spirit realm has been influenced by Adam and Eve's sin, everything we see and touch here on Earth is affected by the law of sin and death. Everyone who lives or who has ever lived on this Earth is affected by the consequences of sin, which are total and unrelenting. Things go wrong. We are disappointed. People get sick, grow old, and die—Christians too. No perfection exists here. We will have to wait until the next life to see everything put under his feet. Until then we have his promises to help us overcome the spiritual forces that rise up to take our territory. Those same promises can give us victory over the ruinous power of famine.

Because God always deals with his children in love, even when He opposes you there is hope. His plan is not to destroy you but to lead you to repent, which ultimately leads you back to Him. And when you come back to Him, you come back to abundant life.

So if you're tired of sowing much and reaping little, if you suspect God is boxing you in, if you're

ready to hear what you must do to make some good
changes in your life, keep reading. People just like you
have gone through the same distressing situations, and
in their stories the Holy Spirit lights the path to your
restoration. I promise you, by the time you've finished
reading here about famines God has sent to others,
you'll know three things. One, you'll know for certain
that it is God who sends famine. Two, you'll know if
what you're experiencing is a true famine or just an
ordinary faith trial. And three, if it's famine, you'll
know exactly what biblical steps to take to break its
power to destroy you.

2. Haggai: "Consider Your Ways"

*And I called for a drought upon the land, and upon
the mountains, and upon the corn, and upon the new
wine, and upon the oil, and upon that which the ground
bringeth forth, and upon men, and upon cattle, and
upon all the labor of the hands.* Haggai 1:11

When the prophet Haggai spoke these words to the
Jews who had returned from Babylonian captivity to
rebuild the temple in Jerusalem, the project had been
started then ignored for sixteen years. Excited to return
to the familiarity and freedom of their homeland, the
fifty thousand exiles had begun to build with
enthusiasm. But eventually they abandoned the project
when hostile neighbors opposed them.

By the time Haggai came on the scene, the Jews
had silenced the opposition and returned to work. But
the work they returned to was not the work God had
given them: "Is it time for you, O ye, to dwell in your
ceiled houses, and this house lie waste?" (Haggai 1:4).

The Jews had forgotten God's building program. Instead they were devoting their energy and goods to rebuilding their own homes, while the Lord's house fell into decay.

God was annoyed at their spiritual indifference, so He "called for a drought," which had the predictable result of diminishing the Jews' food supply. Note that He not only called for a drought on what they tried to grow in their fields, but He also frustrated "all the labor of the hands." Every enterprise they attempted came up short. Even the wage earner was losing the game.

Ye have sown much, and bring in little; ye eat, but ye have not enough; ye drink, but ye are not filled with drink; ye clothe you, but there is none warm; and he that earneth wages earneth wages to put it into a bag with holes. Haggai 1:6

Got holes in your bag?

The Jews' grinding lack contradicted the prosperity God promised them in Deuteronomy 28:8, so when their harvests began to fail they should have realized something was wrong. God had promised to command a blessing "in all thou settest thine hand unto." A drought on land, livestock, and people is easy to picture. It means no rain or very little rain. And that means small harvests, barely enough for your own needs today, nothing to set aside for tomorrow, and nothing to share with the poor. With no abundance stored in their barns, they had nothing with which to trade and no means to expand. They needed every mouthful to keep them alive until the next harvest. They were just existing.

But a drought on the "work of the hands" is more far reaching. It means failure to succeed not only in your finances but in everything you attempt. It is frustration and defeat in every endeavor. For the Jews that meant a curse on their fields, food, drink, clothing, wages—their total supply. This is failure to prosper in the material realm. *The material realm is the first area from which God removes his blessing when his people put their own interests above his.*

For you, failure to prosper materially might be any of these scenarios: It's the beautiful home you thought would sell overnight—there's no reason why it shouldn't—but it doesn't sell and it doesn't sell and you're losing money by the bucketful. It's job application after job application that nets you nothing but disappointment. Every job looks like a sure thing; you are so qualified! But strangely, now you don't even get interviews. It doesn't make sense. It means that, though you honestly try, you can't manage to store up anything in your barn-bank to start a business or buy a piece of property, both of which are tools to build wealth. You're just existing, never growing, in the material realm. Or what used to come easily now comes with difficulty or doesn't come at all. You do everything to make it work, but something beyond your control gets in the way of success. You're sowing, doing what you know is necessary to bring harvest, but you're not reaping like you used to. Sound familiar? Read on.

Because the Jews had the promise of across-the-board blessings, you would think that their failure to prosper would get their attention. After all, God designed the drought to do this. It should have caused them to reflect on their ways, it should have provoked them to search themselves for the spiritual explanation for their chronically poor harvests and inability to get ahead. But that was not the case. Left to themselves, the Jews failed to make the connection between their neglect of spiritual duty and their grinding failure and lack. They had become spiritually dull, indifferent to the things of God, and had forgotten his promise. Likely they looked at the cloudless sky and blamed their poor crops on the obvious: lack of rain. But drought was only the symptom of spiritual sickness, evidence of the virus of indifference that had infected their souls. If they had been spiritually healthy they would have asked God why He had stopped the rain, because verse 11 (chapter opening) makes it plain that the God who has many times promised to bless his people with ample rain is the same God who at times withholds it. They had become carnal minded, viewing their condition only through the foggy lens of the natural eye. God had to send Haggai to plainly spell out cause and effect.

Modern Christians can miss this vital connection. We may not realize that our failure to prosper in natural things is a direct result of our failure to prosper in spiritual things. (Again, this is not to say that the godly won't suffer setbacks. But a true famine experience has hallmarks that set it apart from ordinary tests and trials. Keep reading to learn how to recognize them.) We think God's use of famine to discipline his people is strictly an Old Testament phenomenon. We assume that under grace we do not suffer Old Testament-like effects of our disobedience. When famine conditions begin to take hold, we don't look for a spiritual explanation.

Instead we blame our problems on whatever natural symptoms we see with our carnal eyes. We use worldly reasoning to make sense of our predicament. And we don't expect across-the-board blessings on the work of our hands—a big mistake.

We are ignorant of two things. First, because we don't see failure and lack as spiritual problems, we turn our attention to the natural symptoms Satan has inflicted on us (or that we have inflicted on ourselves) and think our struggle is with them. Second, because we think our problems are natural in origin, we pull out our best, natural defenses, usually humanistic responses. But when we look to natural circumstances to explain our poor condition, we are doomed to stay in that condition, because we can't fight spiritual battles with natural weapons and win. Using natural weapons to fight spiritual battles leads to exhaustion, frustration, and disappointment.

We have many excuses for failure, many cloudless skies we blame for lack of harvests in our lives. "I didn't get enough education." "I've never been good at job interviews." "There aren't opportunities to do well in business like there used to be." "We live in an economically depressed area." "My boss won't let me take the training classes I need to get ahead." "I should have had (fewer) kids earlier (later, farther apart, not at all)." "You can't expect to go far when you're Black (female, speak with an accent, over 55, overweight, wear glasses ...)."

None of these natural conditions voids God's promises to prosper you. They have no intrinsic power to block God's blessing. However, if you believe they have power to stop God's hand, then you give them power. Their power is only *perceived* power—which can be powerful indeed. Because when you give yourself permission to fail, you deny the validity of his covenant, and when that happens, faith goes out the window. It's by faith that you receive everything from God. You are saved by faith. You succeed and prosper by faith.

Do the famine conditions recorded in Haggai sound familiar? They weren't starving, just never satisfied. They weren't naked, just never warm enough. They sowed much seed and expected large harvests, but their half-empty barns disappointed them. They had jobs, but their earnings were nibbled away by unexpected expenses, enough so they were never able to put anything aside. Haggai said in 1:9 that they "looked for much, and, lo, it came to little." Why did they look for much? Because they had sowed much, they had worked hard. Reasonably, therefore, each year they expected to do better than the year before, but their expectations, again and again, turned to disappointment. Hard work wasn't enough.

Even their offerings weren't blessed. In Haggai 2:11–14 God explained this by posing a rhetorical question to the priests: If one carries holy flesh (a meat offering) in the pocket of sanctified clothing, and that clothing touches ordinary food, does the ordinary food become holy? Of course not, replied the priests. But, said God, if someone who is ceremonially unclean (according to Old Testament law) touches ordinary food, does the food become unclean? Yes, said the priests.

Then Haggai answered: "So is this people, and so is this nation before me, saith the Lord; and so is every

15

work of their hands; and that which they offer there is unclean." (2:14)

What the Jews were doing was giving God's ten percent, the tithe, back to Him and giving freewill offerings from the ninety percent of all their increase as they had been taught, but because their hearts weren't right He didn't receive what they gave and didn't bless them in return. They didn't understand that it isn't enough just to do the mechanics, to perform religious exercises. God is looking for sanctified hearts.

In modern terms, we would say they just couldn't get ahead. For you this would be like working overtime, expecting the extra dollars to make a difference in your lifestyle, but it never does because little disasters come along to eat them up. It's expecting a promotion because you've been so conscientious about doing exemplary work, but you get passed over. It's looking at your income tax statement and realizing you're earning more money than you ever have, but your savings account and spending cash look as pathetic as they did five years ago. Every January you say to yourself that this is the year you will get out of debt, but you don't. You work hard but don't get anywhere. You think to yourself, "No matter what I bring home, it's never enough." Nothing you do succeeds, and your failures aren't limited to the financial realm. You're sowing much but reaping little. During the long years of famine in our house, my husband and I tithed and gave offerings as before, but it didn't make a bit of difference. The windows of Heaven were shut to us.

Maybe you wouldn't call your condition famine. That sounds extreme to you. And maybe you'd say that, while the Jews' financial condition sounds sorry

16

enough, it was not a famine as we normally define it.
Well you'd be right about that second part. God's
mercy kept them from the brunt of a ruinous, full-
fledged, howling famine. Yet there is a truth here that is
vital to understanding how God uses famine to deal
with his people now as well as in biblical times.

As with New Testament Christians, God had
promised to bless the Jews materially, and He had never
revoked his promise. So when God put the big squeeze
on their natural supply, He did so to wake them up. The
famine they suffered was a result of something they had
failed to do; it was a reaction on God's part to a sin of
omission on their part. Famine is never an arbitrary
condition. There is always a reason. God doesn't send
famine to you one morning because He got up on the
wrong side of the bed. We must always look to
ourselves and "consider our ways" when we begin to
experience famine. When the Jews suffered lack instead
of experiencing prosperity, they should have
immediately asked themselves what they were doing or
not doing that kept back abundance. They should have
expected an abundant lifestyle. They should have
expected God to rebuke the devourer. (Malachi 3:11)
They should have expected to prosper.

God said in Haggai 1:9, "Ye looked for much, and,
lo, it came to little; and when ye brought it home, I did
blow upon it," or rather, He blew it away. Is something,
or someone, blowing away your earnings? What are
you doing? What are you getting?

Meditate on this: God told them to "consider their
ways," that is, to contemplate their current natural
condition, the insufficiency of their supply. For
emphasis He repeated his command (Haggai 1:5–7),

each time directing them to think about their poor harvests, poor clothing, and empty money bags. It's as if God was saying, "Don't you see I'm no longer blessing you? Don't you realize your lack means there's a problem here? That your poor financial condition is abnormal?" His concern for their material prosperity refutes critics who suggest that God takes little interest in the material well-being of his people.

God was telling them to read the headlines of their lives. Bad news gets people's attention, that's why bad news sells newspapers. Stories about everyday occurrences are more desirable, of course, but they're boring because they are the expected order of things. We expect the sun to shine in summer; we expect the majority of people to roll out of bed each morning and go to work; we expect Christmas to arrive every year on December 25. We don't buy newspapers to read about expected, ordinary events. Stories that grab readers' attention are those we don't expect: tidal waves, a drastic fall in the stock market, shocking crimes, presidents who play hanky-panky with nubile White House interns. Editors put salacious stories on the front page because they know that out-of-the-ordinary headlines make us stop, buy, and read.

God used the same method to get the Jews' attention. He stopped blessing their natural supply, which brought about conditions opposite of what He had promised would be their everyday experience. Because they had taken their focus off spiritual things and put it on natural things, it's those areas that God had to touch to get their attention. He succeeded too. When Haggai spoke of their poor finances, they listened. The well-being of our pocketbooks is of interest to us all. The Jews were no exception.

Haggai's preaching on spiritual consequences was neither new nor unique. God used this painful method to provoke his people to repentance long before Haggai came along. Around a thousand years before Haggai prophesied to the Jews, Moses wrote in Deuteronomy of the specific methods God would use to discipline his people if they ran after foreign gods:

Then the LORD's anger will burn against you, and he will shut the heavens so that it will not rain and the ground will yield no produce, and you will soon perish from the good land the LORD is giving you. Deuteronomy 11:17

And,

You will sow much seed in the field but you will harvest little, because locusts will devour it. Deuteronomy 28:38

This disobedience-and-curse scenario is repeated throughout the Old Testament. Though the word *famine* does not always appear in the text, the result is the same. God warned that pestilence, drought, and sword would hound the disobedient again and again. A particularly chilling and lengthy prophecy along these lines is found in Jeremiah chapters 6 and 7. Every word came to pass.

Christians enjoy a better covenant than Old Testament Jews. But Old Testament stories were written to instruct us, that we might understand the characteristics of God and how He deals with his people. Knowing these truths leads us to a foundational truth: *Prosperity and success as an everyday experience is God's plan for us; lack and failure are aberrations.* God used lack and failure then only to get their attention; He uses it now to get ours as well. Having enough of this world's material goods to be comfortable and some to share is an inherited right and reasonable expectation of every Christian. When the Holy Spirit leads us into any venture, we should, despite inevitable challenges to our faith, expect it to succeed. If you want to believe God for far more wealth than is necessary to secure comfort, for whatever reason, that's your business and your privilege. But it is a fact that Jesus died on the cross not only to save you from your sins but also to break the *results* of sin off your life, which include chronic lack and failure.

If prosperity and success are not our reasonable, everyday experience, if we can expect to only scratch along, in debt, getting our minimum needs met, living paycheck to paycheck, having nothing to share with others, never enjoying abundance in our barn-banks as the Jews in the book of Haggai, never having our dreams for ministry or career realized, suffering the fall-out of broken relationships, if frustration and disappointment were the norm for God's people then and us now, then God used a very strange way to get the Jews' attention. If just getting by was meant to be their everyday experience, then Haggai's message made no sense.

If prosperity and success are not evident there is often, but not always, a problem in the spiritual realm. If our spiritual house is in order—we're prospering in our spirit, growing in love and the knowledge of God's

20

word—prosperity in our spirit will reflect outward into the natural realm. Truly, the kingdom of God is *within us*. As we live out of the abundance we sow into our spirit we enjoy success in whatever we put our hand to (but we should make sure we are putting our hand to something!). Because as we live and move in Him, He directs our pursuits and leads us to the victories He's already won for us.

The Jews did not have the continuous indwelling Spirit of God as we do, but they had specific promises regarding prosperity and the work of their hands. Sadly they neglected his word as well as his house, and that's why God sent Haggai. Though they were slow to catch on, they did repent (after Haggai twice made his case), because failure and lack are effective tools to inspire behavioral change. When they began to put the construction of his house above their own, God began to send abundance. But a long break in their prosperity was not God's idea. They brought it upon themselves by disobedience and spiritual sloth.

The same God who took offense at his people then for putting their work above his warns us now not to make their mistake. "Seek ye first the kingdom of God, and his righteousness," Jesus said, "and all these things shall be added unto you" (Matthew 6:33). "These things" Jesus spoke of are the things all people hope to have plenty of: food, clothing, adequate housing, and whatever else it takes to be comfortable. But the Jews to whom Haggai was sent had devoted their best efforts, time, and supplies to building their own little kingdoms. You would think that by pouring the best of what they had into worldly pursuits they'd enjoy the best of worldly comforts. And yet that was exactly the area where they failed to prosper. They had their priorities wrong, and God won't bless any work that we exalt above his own. Without his blessing, famine results, because in Him we live and move and have our being. We can do nothing without Him.

When lack and failure settled in for a long, undisturbed siege, in their spiritual dullness they shamefully just let it happen. God sent famine because of their wrong priorities, but they let it prevail for sixteen miserable years because they had forgotten his promises. Even then, they still didn't grasp the spiritual aspect of cause and effect, so God had to send Haggai to point it out, plainly and repeatedly. Their sin may not seem particularly egregious: at the outset it appears nothing more sinister than a little nap on the job or that they had temporarily misdirected their spiritual focus. At first glance these oversights or misjudgments may not appear as weighty a sin as greed, fornication, or murder. But God weighed their priorities in his heavenly scale and found their love for Him and his kingdom too light to be acceptable.

When it comes to our response to his love, God hates indifference.

We too should consider our ways. We should wake up and consider what we are doing and what we are getting. If you've read this far, you are awake. You're one of the few who is alert enough to realize all is not right. Life should be better; you had expected more. Fortunately for you, not all Bible characters responded foolishly to famine. One man in particular considered his ways and in doing so provides us a good example of how to spiritually interpret famine-like circumstances.

3. David Inquires of the Lord

Then there was a famine in the days of David three years, year after year; and David inquired of the Lord. And the Lord answered, It is for Saul and for his bloody house, because he slew the Gibeonites. II Samuel 21:1

It's amazing how the Holy Spirit packs so much knowledge into one verse. Four truths about famine are tucked into these thirty-nine words and a fifth is hidden later in the passage. Yet all along we've thought this was just another quaint little story about King David and his on-again, off-again troubles with Saul and his legacy of rebellion.

Truth number one: *Famine works over a long period.*

Why did David allow Israel to suffer through three years of famine before he asked God the cause of it? Why did he wait so long? Shouldn't one bad year have been long enough to alert David of a problem?

David waited to seek God because one bad year, one downturn, is not evidence of a famine. Famine is evidenced over the long haul, usually several but never

23

longer than seven years. After three years of poor harvests, David saw a trend, began to suspect famine, and wisely searched for the cause on his knees. His people faced hunger, and as a caring leader, this fact alone would have sent him to his knees even if he hadn't suspected God was behind the famine. He knew something was not right, and He knew who would tell him what was wrong and what to do about it. But most important, he knew there was a spiritual answer to a natural problem.

You *should not*, however, interpret every setback on your path to success to be a famine sent by God. A setback in your plans might mean only that perhaps you missed God's direction along the way. It could mean Satan is trying to block you from receiving what is rightfully yours. Jesus told us to expect tribulation. The enemy isn't going to hand over territory without a fight and he'll do anything to steal God's word from your heart. It could mean God is drawing you to a higher level of faith. Or maybe it's just that your timing and God's are opposed. A setback can mean a lot of things. But it doesn't always mean famine and, in fact, most of the time it does not. Temporary setbacks are a part of living in a fallen world. Resist them. Resist also the temptation to see them as anything more spiritually sinister than stubbed toes in the long-distance race of faith.

You should experience a gradual but steady climb *upward* toward your goals. If what you experience is a gradual, steady slide *downward* toward failure, then it's time to start asking God why. That's what David did.

Truth number two: *There is always a reason for famine.*

The Bible does not say what famine symptoms David and his people experienced. We don't know if it was drought, pestilence, soil problems, theft by armed marauders (this happened in Gideon's time) or whatever, because the bottom line is we don't need to know the means. Only the cause and solution are important. The means of famine is the least important factor because, as you saw in chapter one, the means of famine vary for everyone: the opera singer, the farmer, the evangelist—you too. God will use the unique circumstances that surround *you* to get your attention. What we need to know is that God's promised abundance did not materialize and that David saw the symptoms of famine as a red flag, an alert to pray, because David expected God to prosper his people. You too will see the red flag waving with your spiritual eyes. Perhaps it's been waving in your life for some time and that's why you picked up this book. My red flag was the day after my house foreclosed when the Realtor called to tell us that seven offers for our home had arrived on her desk twenty-four hours too late to rescue us. Seven!

And people accuse God of being silent.

So David inquired of the Lord as to the reason for the famine. Though the Bible does not record the actual words David spoke, it could only have been "Why, Lord?" because the response God gave him answered this question. Some Christians have a problem with asking God why because they've been taught that doing so is presumptuous. They've been taught that asking why is to question God's judgment, revealing a lack of trust in God's goodness and justice. To them, asking why is akin to "putting forth a fleece" or "asking for a sign." Their interpretation of scripture presupposes that God is not interested in telling us why He does what He does and that our involvement with Him is strictly passive. More simply, they would ask, "Why do we need to know why God does what He does? He's going to do it anyway, and knowing why does not affect what we do one way or the other." They like to quote Job, "Shall we receive good at the hand of God, and shall we not receive evil?" (Job 2:10) Yet Job asked God why, and God answered him. God also revealed his ways (and thoughts and reasoning) to Moses. Christians who have trouble with asking why think that our responsibility as servants is merely to receive his dealings with faith, trust, and unquestioning obedience. There is no room for why.

This interpretation is faulty in several ways. First, if David had subscribed to it Israel would have been wiped out (unless, of course, God had sent another Haggai along). Second, we have an enemy who tries to thwart God's plan for us, and what we interpret as God's dealings may be Satan's tricks, which God has commanded us to resist. Third, famine contradicts God's promises of material blessings. Famine is a curse, therefore, when it manifests there has to be a reason. "The curse causeless shall not come." (Proverbs 26:2) Knowing these things emboldened David and led him to the only logical conclusion: he had to seek God for a reason for the famine. His reasoning went like this: Something is wrong. God must be involved. What must we do to fix it?

Going to God for the answer was his wisest course of action as a leader. David assumed God is involved in the daily affairs of his people, that their actions move

Him, and that his actions affect them. Because the material world is the result of a decision first made in the spiritual realm—God spoke and the world was created—so too the material world is under the thumb of the spiritual. We forget this sometimes, but David did not forget. He figured rightly, and God answered him without delay, showing him the connection between Saul's sin and the famine.

And God did not rebuke David for asking.

Truth number three: *You should go to God first to find the reason for famine.*

In the midst of famine David kept a spiritual focus. He went straight to God for an explanation of the famine. He did not look to the sky (no rain), the earth (bad soil), the rate of inflation (economic trends beyond his control), the gross national product (no one else seems to be making much money), or the kingdom employment rate (I'm no worse off than anyone else) to explain Israel's downturn. People will give you bad counsel. To explain your troubles they will make false assumptions about you, your ability, and your circumstances that not even *you* had thought of. But usually they'll look to the obvious (cloudless skies) and assign a natural explanation for your failure to prosper. Through the prophet Isaiah, God condemned the practice of his people who ran to "wizards that peep, and that mutter." Instead, God asked, "Should not a people seek unto their God?" (Isaiah 8:19)

God is quick to answer you when you come to Him in honesty, with a pure heart, genuinely seeking his mind regarding your trouble. He should be the first you run to because our omniscient Lord is the only one who knows the full extent of what's going on in your life.

God sees the whole picture. One thing you can be sure of, if you seek God to determine if what you're experiencing is a famine He has sent, He'll show you, because God's intent in sending famine is to bring your attention back on Him, something He's anxious to do. When He's brought you to that desired point, He won't abandon you to confusion.

If you seek Him on your own and still don't have a clear picture of your situation, then it's time to visit a Spirit-filled counselor who regularly hears from God. Men and women who move in the Spirit realm act as God's mouthpieces. Their counsel can be invaluable, especially when you are young in the Lord. Often they see things that need to change in your life that you are blind to.

Truth number four: *You may suffer famine because of someone else's sin.*

Ouch! This truth is obvious, and obviously painful to experience. But it's important to understand how it can affect you personally. For David this meant watching his people suffer for a season, hurting when they hurt. *Yet David and the rest of Israel had done nothing to cause famine.* God sent the famine to Israel because of Saul, now dead, who had murdered the Gibeonites, a people to whom Joshua had earlier sworn by treaty not to harm in exchange for their servitude. (Joshua 9:15–21) David was not party to the treaty or the murder, yet the famine arrived during his reign. Fortunately for Israel her leader was spiritually astute and knew where to turn before starvation and death set in. Perhaps that is why God sent famine when He did, because He knew the prayer of Israel's godly king would turn away destruction.

David asked the Gibeonites what they required to atone for Saul's sin, and they demanded seven of Saul's sons be executed. So David turned the young men over to the Gibeonites, who hanged them. II Samuel 21:14 says the executions satisfied God's call for justice, and He was "entreated for the land," meaning He heard his people's prayers and removed the famine.

Here is the good and the bad. As you look at your frustrating circumstances, it may be that you know, deep in your heart, you have done nothing wrong to cause the disasters that keep overtaking you. Perhaps you have sought God, likely over and over again, repenting of everything you could possibly be guilty of, and even of some things you're not. "What have I done? Where have I missed it? Am I totally outside God's will?" you have agonized. After all this soul searching and endless repenting, you're still confused about why so many bad things have happened to you and why your prayers for deliverance go unanswered. Maybe you know you haven't done anything wrong, but suspect that your spouse isn't serving God as he or she ought to. Maybe your entire family is suffering spiritually as a result. This is the bad part. The good part comes next.

Truth number five: *Famine travels behind unanswered prayer.*

This doesn't sound good at the outset, but keep reading.

It wasn't until the bones of Saul's seven sons, and Saul's and Jonathan's bones, were buried that we see a change in Israel's fortune. Once David had fulfilled these demands (II Samuel 21:14) God was "entreated" for the land. "Entreat" is an old-fashioned word that means to make an earnest request, to petition, which is exactly what David and Israel had been doing all along ("year after year" says I Samuel 21:1)—entreating God to deliver them from the famine. Don't you think that, after experiencing a poor harvest the first year, David and the people prayed for God to bless their crops? Do you think they prayed after the second bad harvest? Surely they prayed even harder. And after the third year of crop failure, likely they were praying around the clock.

But here is a chilling fact: God heard but refused to answer. He refused to be entreated because *they were praying the wrong way.* They were praying for abundant harvests, but that is not the prayer God was waiting to hear. It wasn't until David inquired as to *why* the famine had manifested that God spoke, and the famine wasn't removed until God's people executed justice for the Gibeonites. So it was critical that someone, in this case David, had the boldness to pray and ask God why. Never forget this.

Often when we pray for improvement in our desperate situation, which has been brought about by famine, God is waiting to reveal what caused our suffering in the first place so we can correct it. Because we don't realize we are causing our own pain, we hope that through prayer God will change his mind about what He's allowing in our lives. We want Him to deal with the effects but not the cause, or, we mistakenly think his (alleged) capricious will is the cause. ("One day He blesses me, one day He doesn't.") Meanwhile we go through endless agony as we pray over and over again for painful symptoms to be removed. We're waiting for Him; He's waiting for us. Observing

Israel's frustrating, desperate experience should inspire holy fear in every Christian's heart. *When you stand at the brink of disaster and your cries to God go unheeded, pay attention!* Alarm bells should go off in your spirit (Red flag! Red flag!) and drive you to inquire of God, because it might be time to change your prayers, as David did. It could be that God is only waiting for someone to pray the right prayer. And that person could be you.

I know because I've been there. As I mentioned earlier, I've known the agony of unanswered prayer as I faced one of the worst deadlines of my life: the last day the lender had given us to make all our delinquent mortgage payments or lose our house. Though I cried wildly and loudly to God for deliverance, He refused to help. I might as well have been praying to my computer for all the response I got from Heaven. The deadline came and went and we faced our disaster without the help I thought was due us. It's still painful to even think about that fateful day, let alone share such a dark episode with you on these pages. My response to our evil circumstances was all wrong. I was praying for rain when I should have been asking why the drought.

But here's what I learned, the good part I promised you. Though your home has been troubled by evil circumstances beyond your control, you may be the David whom God has raised up to intercede for yourself and those you love. The fact that you're holding this book in your hands is hope itself, because you're spiritually astute enough to discern that things are not right, that there must be a spiritual solution to your problems. God is the answer, but you must ask the right question. You decided some time ago that life

31

should be better than this, that you can expect more of God, so you're searching for an explanation and a solution. That's hope speaking, and you're listening.

I want to encourage you that by asking *Why?* you're doing the right thing. Unanswered prayer should drive us to ask why, especially unanswered prayer in the face of disaster, a critical deadline. Someone once said, "If you keep on doing what you've been doing, you're gonna keep on getting what you've been getting." If for too long, year after year, you've been praying the same old prayers about your desperate situation, but your situation just gets more desperate, it's time to stop and consider your ways. Maybe you need to pray differently.

Some prayers require more time to be answered, of course, such as when we pray for salvation of loved ones. But other prayers demand an immediate answer, as in Israel's case when they faced extinction by starvation. I won't belabor the point; I think you know the difference between the two. You know when you need God to deliver you now and when you're just tired of persevering.

If you recognize yourself and your circumstances in this story, now you have David's example to show you what to do. Pray that God will show you what problem in your life has caused the famine, and pray that He'll show what steps you must take to fix it. God designed this painful correction to get your attention. He is waiting to hear from you.

4. Elimelech Brings His Famine to Moab

No hiding place exists for you if God sends a
famine into your life, because famine is not an
experience limited to a geographical area. Famine is a
condition of the spirit reflected outward into the natural
realm. Famine is a heart condition; it goes where you
go. This is true also of Old Testament famines, though
at first glance these appear to be conditions limited to a
specific region on a map. If that were so, however, then
God's people could have easily escaped his dealings by
pulling up their tent pegs, loading up their camels, and
caravaning across the desert to a better watering hole.

We cannot outsmart God.

But some try. The Book of Ruth tells the story of
Elimelech, a man who tried to outrun a famine and
failed. He lived during the time of the Judges in
Bethlehem-Judah with his wife Naomi and two sons. It
was a period of unrest for the Israelites, when their
spiritual backbone was weakened by foreign enemies,

tribal jealousies, and idolatry. When famine came upon
the land, Elimelech decided without God's counsel that
the only way to save his family from starvation was to
flee Israel and join the Moabites, an idolatrous nation
that God had told the Israelites to have nothing to do
with.

Elimelech and his family lived in Moab about ten
years. Though Elimelech found enough food there to
sustain his family, the tragic record the Holy Spirit left
of this man's life tells us that physical nourishment was
the only comfort he enjoyed. During that decade
Elimelech died. After his death, his sons married
Moabite women, unions God had forbidden and
Elimelech surely would not have approved. Both sons
died childless. We infer that they died immediately
after marriage, before their wives could conceive, or
possibly God shut their wives' wombs. Both scenarios
reek of a curse. Personally, I believe God intervened
because He didn't want Abraham's descendants setting
down roots in Moab. Regardless, by removing himself
and his family to Moab, Elimelech's line was cut off,
the very thing he feared would happen to him if he
remained in Israel. What's more, his wife was left
alone, bereaved, in a strange land, of a strange
language, of strange gods, with no male relatives to
support her. She became a destitute widow, a little
higher on the social ladder than a leper.

Death for him and desperation for her were the
antithesis of Elimelech's plan when he fled Israel for
greener grass. He thought he was escaping disaster, *but
the famine was upon him and his people,* not upon a
plot of land in Israel. Where Elimelech went, the
famine went too.

The same tragic scenario is depicted in Jeremiah 24, wherein destruction followed the Israelites who tried to do an end run around God's justice by fleeing to Egypt before Nebuchadnezzar's army invaded Jerusalem. God promised that they would not outrun his judgment.

So will I give Zedekiah the king of Judah, and his princes, and the residue of Jerusalem, that remain in this land, and them that dwell in the land of Egypt.

And I will deliver them to be removed into all the kingdoms of the earth for their hurt, to be a reproach and a proverb, a taunt and a curse, in all places whither I shall drive them.

And I will send the sword, the famine, and the pestilence, among them, till they be consumed from off the land that I gave unto them and to their fathers. Jeremiah 24:8–10 (emphasis mine)

When Naomi found herself alone in Moab (alone except for Ruth, not a blood relative nor a Hebrew) she did not immediately return to Israel to live again among God's people, although she had friends there and at least two male relatives. Instead she was content to live among the heathen. She returned to her homeland only when she heard the famine there had ended. This fact, and what we already know about what motivated Elimelech, is a disturbing commentary on this couple's priorities. Elimelech abandoned Israel of his own accord (unlike Jacob and Isaac whom God told to leave their countries during famine), refused to submit to God's dealing, chose to live among idolaters, and risked his children's spiritual welfare for material comfort. His

wife's actions reflect the same worldly priorities.
Naomi returned to Israel only when she heard that her
people had food.

That's sad. But the saddest of all is that this
family's painful, permanent loss was unnecessary.
Israel was not wiped out by the famine. When Naomi
heard in Moab that God had "visited his people in
giving them bread," (Ruth 1:6) she and her daughter-in-
law Ruth returned to Bethlehem, and "All the city was
moved about them, and they said, 'Is this Naomi?'"
(Ruth 1:19) If the whole city turned out for their
homecoming, they weren't dead as Elimelech had
presumed would be their fate. And note that the women
who greeted them recognized Naomi. They called her
by name. They were the same friends and neighbors she
had left behind ten years earlier, not newcomers on the
block since the famine retreated. Had Naomi and her
family stayed behind and submitted to God's dealing,
by his mercy they too would have survived.

We'll never know if Elimelech, before his death,
discerned his error. But we know Naomi finally came to
understand that God was behind the hard dealings with
this family, that their sufferings had been under his
control and by his direction. Though some cannot
receive this truth and would question God's goodness,
for others it is a witness to his compassion. His faithful
dealings are our singular hope. Listen to her testimony:

*And it came to pass, when they were come to
Bethlehem, that all the city was moved about them, and
they said, Is this Naomi?*
*And she said unto them, Call me not Naomi, call
me Mara: for the Almighty hath dealt very bitterly with*

me.
I went out full, and the Lord hath brought me home
again empty. Ruth 1:19-21

Note her telling confession: *She* brought *herself*
"out" (of Israel) but *He* brought her back in. God is
merciful. He who takes away also gives back. Though
Naomi came back to Israel only because food was
available there, once she made the decision to return to
the land God had chosen as a dwelling place for her and
her people, blessing upon blessing came into her life.
Ruth proved her love and faithfulness to Naomi once
again, beyond her initial demonstration of devotion in
accompanying her mother-in-law to Israel, by working
long hours in the hot sun—as a man would—to support
them both. Then Boaz graciously took over the
financial burden for the widows, and we know how
Ruth became David's great-grandmother and was
honored to be grafted into the lineage of Jesus Christ.
God is more gracious than we can imagine: By Ruth's
gift of Obed, Elimelech and Naomi were also honored
to be a part of that lineage. (4:10) In short, when Naomi
returned to her place and people where God had desired
her to dwell all along, He restored all that Satan had
taken from her: family, heritage, and material supply.
These were the very things Elimelech hoped to preserve
when he set out to live among the heathen. He just went
about it the wrong way.

So what is the moral to this story? If God sends
you famine, you can't outrun it. You may blame your
failure to prosper on the economy, your supervisor, the
area where you live, your parents or background, your
spouse. When you do, you'll be tempted to change what

you can, usually to your loss. No effort on your part will remove the famine, because the famine isn't on these things, it's on you. So whatever new circumstance you create for yourself to reduce the pain—new city, new supervisor, new home, new spouse—in the end none of these will bring the success you seek. The famine will manifest in your new situation just like it did in the old until you seek God, find out what the real problem is, and fix it.

Because they regard not the works of the Lord, nor the operation of his hands, he shall destroy them, and not build them up. Psalm 28:5

5. Famine Is for the Disobedient

If your heart is right with God and you're living in his word, you have nothing to fear from famine, because famine is for the disobedient. God has promised to feed his people during natural famines (Psalms 33:18–19; 37:18–19) and we have Bible examples of how God's people were surrounded by famine yet prospered. His laws and promises work the same way in the spirit realm for us now.

Three Bible patriarchs lived during times of famine. They were not only unharmed by the destruction around them but became rich by God's blessing.

Abraham. Genesis 12 tells Abraham's story. At God's command Abraham (then called Abram) departed Haran for Canaan, but sometime after he arrived famine gripped the land, and Abraham feared for the welfare of himself and his family. So he packed up his family and belongings and headed for Egypt, although the Bible does not record that God told him to do this. Because of his wife's extraordinary beauty, Abraham feared the Egyptians would take her and kill him, so he told his wife to tell everyone she was his sister. The Egyptians did take Sarah, but when Pharaoh discovered she was married to Abraham, he thrust both of them and their household out of the country. When Abraham left, the Bible records in Genesis 13:2, he was "very rich" in cattle, silver, and gold, likely appropriated from the Egyptians who were anxious to expel him from the land. His nephew, Lot, was also exceedingly wealthy, so much so that when they returned to Canaan, the land was not able to support their combined flocks and herds. (Genesis 13:6)

Isaac. Isaac also prospered during famine. After Abraham died a second famine arose in Canaan, and Isaac, grown and married to Rebekah, decided to pull up stakes just as his father had done and move out of the area to find food. And like his father, he purposed to go to Egypt. But God spoke to him (Genesis 26:2) and told him to stay in the Gentile land of Gerar of the Philistines. "In this land," He said, "I will be with thee, and will bless thee." So Isaac stayed, tilled the ground, and in a year of famine reaped a hundred-fold return. (Genesis 26:12) In fact, Isaac's herds, crops, and servants multiplied so quickly and so exponentially that the Philistines envied him in an unfriendly way. (Genesis 26:14) Abimelech, king of the Philistines, recognizing that Isaac's household had become mightier than all his people combined, urged Isaac to leave. So Isaac and his household left, but not before they had eaten the best of the Gentile lands: God's provision during famine. As we saw in Abraham's case, God used Gentiles to fulfill his purposes by having them provoke his people to return to their inheritance. He didn't want them to set down roots, to become comfortable living among the wicked.

Jacob. As a young man Jacob had an enemy, his evil father-in-law Laban, who was determined to steal from Jacob everything he earned. Jacob suffered twenty years as an employee of Laban, who lied to him, changed his wages ten times (Genesis 31:7), sold his own daughters (Jacob's wives) and devoured their money (Genesis 31:15), and was of such wicked nature that Jacob feared he would even take away his wives. (Genesis 31:31) God thwarted Laban's evil plans and showed Jacob how to more than win back his earnings. When Jacob finally freed himself from his father-in-law's house, he legally took with him nearly all of Laban's herds and flocks, destroying the one who had robbed him. Laban's tricks always failed because God had blessed Jacob with the same blessing with which He had blessed his father Isaac and his grandfather Abraham. The blessing of prosperity that was spoken over Abraham is the same blessing you, as Abraham's descendant, have inherited in Christ.

As an older man Jacob experienced famine as his father and grandfather had before him. In all three cases, God used famine to fulfill his purpose. Jacob was reluctant to move his twelve sons and their families to Egypt, but God assured him in a dream (Genesis 46:3–4) that He had plans to bring his descendants out of Egypt and into the Promised Land. While in Egypt the Israelites, though suffering bondage, grew in such numbers that, once again, they caused the Gentiles to fear and were thrust out of the land, again loaded down with material wealth. As in the cases of Abraham and

Isaac who fled loaded down with the wealth of the unjust, Exodus 12:36 says the Israelites "spoiled" the Egyptians, meaning they "plucked" or "stripped" them. The Egyptians were so anxious to rid themselves of the Israelites that whatever material goods the Israelites requested of the Egyptians before they fled they received. They took so much of the Egyptian's silver and gold with them into the desert that when it was time to take offerings of these items to build the temple, Moses had to tell the people to quit giving because of the excess.

God has even gone out of his way to make sure that just one righteous person was spared the effects of famine because of her faithfulness. II Kings 8 tells the story of the Shunammite woman, the rich but barren believer who built a sleeping room for the prophet Elisha on the roof of her home. For her kindness God blessed her and her husband with a son. When the child died of a sudden illness, Elisha prayed and the boy was raised from the dead. When God called for a famine (II Kings 8:1), Elisha warned her to leave Israel for the duration. By faith she and her family fled the area and dwelt with the Philistines for seven years.

What happened to her when she returned home is significant. God not only spared her life and the lives of her household during famine, but He preserved and restored her possessions as well. When she returned to Canaan she discovered that someone had moved into her house and taken over her fields. Naturally she wanted them back, and so to the king she went to make her case. As she and her son approached the throne, Elisha's servant Gehazi was speaking to the king about Elisha's miraculous works, specifically those involving the Shunammite woman. When Gehazi saw her and her son standing in the throne room, he confirmed to the king that she was the very woman whose son Elisha had raised from the dead. Impressed with Gehazi's testimony, the king ordered an officer of the court to see that she got her house and lands back. Equally important, the king ordered that all the crops her land had yielded while she was away be returned to her. In one day God put back into her hands what Satan had stolen from her for a period of seven years. Actually she was *given* the crops, because she had spent not one day tilling, sowing, or gathering to earn them. God assigned these tasks to someone less worthy.

These biblical examples of God's preservation of the righteous during famine prove three things. First, God differentiates between the obedient and disobedient; He knows if you've been bad or good. Second, if Satan has used famine to steal from you, it is God's plan to fully restore what Satan has taken. And third, famine is for sinners. So if you've been acting more like a sinner than a believer, it's time to repent. Because if you don't repent, I'm here to tell you that there's worse to come than an empty stomach.

6. Famine's Disastrous Work

One of the hardest truths about famine is how wholly destructive it is. Its hallmark is merciless totality; only what God declares shall be spared is spared as it marches through your world, crushing the life out of everything important to you. Famine is more than hunger. Hunger is mere discomfort, but famine is a rapacious spiritual force that devours with frightening appetite. It is the essence of Satan's character in operation because, under God's control, it is Satan himself who performs the deed: stealing, killing, and destroying without warning, indiscriminately and completely.

The Samaritans learned this firsthand. Their land was besieged by the Syrians in II Kings 6. Syria's King Ben-hadad circled his troops around Samaria, cutting off the city's food supply until the people became so hungry that they paid exorbitant prices for what little undesirable food was left (verse 25). Worse, Samaria's citizens had turned to cannibalism of the basest sort, making meals of their own children rather than repent

44

and seek God for relief. Could a people be more spiritually impoverished than this?

Every time I read this story I grieve. I grieve because I know that famine is a spiritual condition we bring upon ourselves. I grieve because Christians needlessly suffer so intensely. I know. I was one of them and I've met others. Though famine is God's work, it is not God's will. If hunger alone would cause us to repent, He'd stop there, but often our nature is so obstinate, our spiritual sleep so heavy, that He has to use his big guns, the ones that discharge with a bigger boom and longer range, to wake us up. It may seem to you when you're in the midst of famine that He's going after a gnat with a cannon, but that's because *He intends* his chastening to be unpleasant. (Hebrews 12:11)

The prodigal son is the classic New Testament example of how painful famine can be. Luke 15 tells the story of this arrogant, impatient young man who grew weary of smelly, dirty farm work and the irksomeness of submitting to his father. This famous upstart yearned for the good life, to be on his own, doing what he wanted, when he wanted, with whom he wanted. So he went to his father and asked for his inheritance. For reasons not disclosed in scripture, the father didn't deny him but divided his estate and gave his younger son his portion. In a hurry to indulge himself with his new wealth, the Bible says in verse 13 that in only a few days he had packed up his belongings and left home.

You know the story. He wasted his inheritance on riotous living, on prostitutes and like individuals and pursuits. Soon a mighty famine broke out upon the

45

land, and he found himself broke, hungry, and jobless. This son of a wealthy landowner was reduced to feeding pigs, an exceedingly lowly job considering that Jews didn't eat pork and were considered spiritually unclean if they so much as touched swine.

Verse 16 is telling. He was so hungry, it says, that he longed to eat even the corn husks he fed to the pigs, "but no man gave unto him." The Holy Spirit could have stopped after telling us how desperately hungry the young man was, but He went further. He noted that no one had pity on him, no one favored him. One of the indicators of a famine operating in your life is that because you don't have favor with God, neither do you have favor with people, which is a gift from God and a primary conduit of his grace. "For thou, Lord, wilt bless the righteous; with favor wilt thou compass him as with a shield." (Psalm 5:12) Many Bible verses speak of God's favor to the righteous and how it expresses itself by favor with people. But God wouldn't favor this young man through others because God's design was to make him miserable—miserable enough to repent.

The whole story turns on the next few verses:

And when he came to himself, he said, How many hired servants of my father's have bread enough and to spare, and I perish with hunger!

I will arise and go to my father, and will say unto him, Father, I have sinned against heaven, and before thee,

And am no more worthy to be called thy son: make me as one of thy hired servants.

And he arose, and came to his father. But when he was yet a great way off, his father saw him, and had compassion, and ran, and fell on his neck, and kissed him. Luke 15:17–20 (emphasis mine)

What was it that brought this young man to repentance? The Holy Spirit makes it easy for us: the son was starving, and the misery of that condition "brought him to himself." He saw himself as he really was, unworthy, but sadly it took the loss of everything to bring him to that knowledge. Famine's work was complete; the prodigal son had a new heart. Gone was the arrogant youth deceived by riches, spiritually handicapped by the notion that his father owed him something. Note what did *not* bring him to repentance: he had shamed his family, reduced his father's estate, squandered his own, and was working as a farmhand, but none of this moved him to repent. It was *hunger* that woke him up spiritually. How hungry was he? Not only was he tempted to eat pig food, but the Bible records in verse 22 that he arrived home shoeless. Likely he had sold his shoes for a meal.

Like others we've seen who recognize that their folly has brought famine into their lives and long to make a sacrifice to show their genuinely changed heart—their repentance—the prodigal son didn't go home without an offering. Shoeless, penniless, and hungry, he recognized that his hands were empty of anything material with which to impress or mollify his father, so he brought the one gift he couldn't carry but now possessed: his love for his father expressed through service. He was, he said, "no more worthy to be called thy son: make me as one of thy hired servants." Of course, like our heavenly Father, the earthly one wasn't interested in debasing his son. When the boy came home and submitted to his father he was treated like a prince.

What do we learn from this story? Don't wait until you're tempted to do something evil to thwart God's famine in your life. Whatever plan you think up to get out of the mess you're in won't work anyway. If your life is in such disarray that even pig slop looks better than what you've been dining on lately, then it's time to climb out of that trough and head back to where the chow is not only good, it's divine.

You know what to do.

7. Joel's Secret

If you're convinced that God has sent a famine into your life, then you're in the best position you've been in for a long time. You're anxious to find out what you must do to end the misery, so you're listening for direction and poised to act. I have good news for you. God's word is clear regarding the steps you must take to break the famine off your life and turn your situation around, and once you do your part, He is quick to do his.

The Book of Joel outlines your steps to freedom. God spoke to Joel during a grievous time in Israel's history. Scholars disagree about the exact period in which Joel was sent to prophesy his message of hope to Israel, either during Joash's reign around 800 B.C., or a post-Exilic date, around 400 B.C. Regardless, the facts of the story are not disputed. God's disobedient people had been thoroughly ruined by pestilence, which led to famine. The Bible says, "That which the palmerworm hath left hath the locust eaten; and that which the locust

49

hath left hath the cankerworm eaten; and that which the cankerworm hath left hath the caterpillar eaten." (Joel 1:4)

Similar to my family's experience after we moved to Virginia, just when the Israelites thought there would be a little respite from the first plague, then came the second, then the third, then the fourth, until they faced total destruction, which of course, God had to arrange for them because the doom-and-gloom prophecies He had sent earlier had failed to move them to repent. In Joel 1:5–12 Joel laments the total loss of the harvests, right down to the bark on the trees (verse 7).

The secret of Joel isn't so much a truth that God has hidden as it is an understanding that comes only to those who have experienced his dealings. If your famine ordeal has matured you as He planned, you'll understand and receive Joel's instruction to the priests in Joel 1:13:

Gird yourselves, and lament, ye priests: howl, ye ministers of the altar: come, lie all night in sackcloth, ye ministers of my God: for the meat offering and the drink offering is withholden from the house of your God.

The harvests were destroyed and the people were starving, but Joel ignored all that and told the priests to intercede to restore something else, something more serious: meat and drink offerings in the temple. Joel delivered to us a great truth. The cause for alarm is not that *you* are suffering. The real problem is that whatever action you've taken (or failed to take) that brought famine into your life has taken a toll on the worship rightly due your King. When the results of your disobedience cause you to fail, He is robbed of the glory He garners from your success. His kingdom, and the impact your failure has had upon it, should be your first concern. Of course, the majority will turn to God when their own kingdoms are suffering, but it's clear here that our priority should mirror God's. We should expand his kingdom first.

Joel instructed the priests to lament and howl—serious intercession—because of the loss of worship caused by the famine. The famine had run its full course; there was nothing left to offer on the altar. Without a means of worship, there was no hope for Israel.

So Joel gave specific instruction: "Sanctify ye a fast, call a solemn assembly, gather the elders and all the inhabitants of the land into the house of the Lord your God, and cry unto the Lord." (Joel 1:14) Joel told the priests, elders, and all the people to fast and cry unto the Lord. Then he got even more specific:

Therefore also now, saith the Lord, turn ye even to me with all your heart, and with fasting, and with weeping, and with mourning:

And rend your heart, and not your garments, and turn unto the Lord your God: for his gracious and merciful, slow to anger, and of great kindness, and repenteth him of the evil.

Who knoweth if he will return and repent, and leave a blessing behind him; even a meat offering and a drink offering unto the Lord your God? Joel 2:12–14

When I was a young Christian, I would read verse

14 and think to myself that if God wanted to "leave a blessing behind" for the starving Israelites, the sensible thing to do would have been to arrange for a few truckloads of peanut butter and jelly sandwiches, several tons of pepperoni pizza, and a couple thousand boxes of crème-filled cupcakes to roll into Jerusalem. A bucket of fried chicken for each family would have been appreciated, I was sure. To my carnal mind the first order of business was dinner for the hungry hordes, not the ministry of the altar.

But that is fleshly thinking. Joel knew what they needed most was to get their priorities right. They needed to 1) "rend their hearts," that is, they needed to repent of their sins, and 2) they needed to take that which was in least supply and offer it in worship to God. Only then would He hear their prayers and bless their harvests. They needed to return to God, to depend on his blessing and not their meager provision. They had to quit looking at the natural. Joel knew there was no other way to prosper.

With their decision to repent and put God's altar before their own stomachs, his plan to feed and care for them was glorious in its completeness. Not only did He promise to bless their land, crops, and livestock, but He promised to restore to them their past, "the years that the locust hath eaten" (Joel 2:25), to prosper them so fully that their future abundance would make them forget they had ever suffered famine. God has a marvelous way of undoing the work of the devil. He can make your future so good (in more than just material items) that you come to the point where the losses of the past don't affect you. It's not that you forget the pain of the past. It's that you're so busy enjoying the blessings of the present that you no longer think about the past. Hence, it loses its power to rob you of your current joy.

That's what God did for me. He spoke words of hope during a very dark period in my life, sometime around early 1995. It was a dark period because I'd been out of the writing field for four years, since March 1991; we'd lost our home in 1993; we were still renting with no foreseeable way to become homeowners again; we were always short of cash and sliding deep into debt as a result; and though we visited fellowship after fellowship, without a church family we were discouraged and depressed. When all I had seen was disappointment and lack for four years, and when I was finding it more difficult than ever to believe for good things, God spoke to me through Joel 2:25 that He had a plan to restore all: "And I will restore to you the years that the locust hath eaten, the cankerworm, and the caterpillar, and the palmerworm, my great army which I sent among you."

I was struck by two truths in this verse: He was going to restore the YEARS to me, and HE had sent a great army of pestilence into our lives. He had been in control of our sufferings and He would be in control of our restoration.

He also told me to fast, which I did, one day a week for months. I understood at that time that it was his plan to restore a home to us, although honestly, I was clueless how He was going to pull this off. By the time God spoke to me that He was going to give us a house, we had lost all the equity in our Alabama home to foreclosure, and we'd been married sixteen years and were the parents of three. We were too old to be renting again after already owning two homes, but there we were, building up some landlord's estate by our rent payments and doing nothing for ourselves financially because we had no equity to put into another house. I kept thinking to myself how our loss was like losing ten years of savings. *Ten years! Ten years!* I would moan to myself. *How will we ever recover?* And then we had a fourth child, making it even harder to save a down payment.

But when God restored a house to us in 1997, FAR better than the house we lost, the new one came fully paid for—no mortgage. So though we lost what felt like ten years, we gained thirty years because the average homeowner signs a thirty-year mortgage note.

God doesn't lie. No matter how large your losses, He will restore to you too what Satan—the greedy, grinding, gluttonous teeth of the locust—has stolen from you during your famine experience. Put God's kingdom first by paying your tithes again and make generous offerings of your money, time, and abilities. He'll replace to you all the years you've lost, just like he did for the Shunammite woman, just like He did for my family. I never think any more about the equity we lost on the old house. I'm too busy thanking Him for our mortgage-free house.

Perhaps you're still not convinced that his grace can turn around your circumstances. Maybe you feel too unworthy to receive, or you've seen so much disappointment that you think you can't believe for change in your life. Or maybe it's just that your offering is so small you find it hard to believe it will impress God. Keep reading. Next is a story of someone less worthy and of less faith than you, yet by her pitiful offering, no more than a mouthful, God delivered her from terrible famine.

8. The Marvel of Faith

There once was a widow who lived, long ago, with her son in the ancient city of Sarepta, a territory of Sidon, now part of southwest Lebanon. Poor, alone, and starving as a result of two years of drought, one day she set about to prepare one last loaf of bread for herself and her son, knowing that when the little bit of flour and oil she had left in the house were gone, they both would soon starve to death. She had resigned herself and her son to this bleak fate. She wasn't depending on God to provide for her because she wasn't a believer. As a Gentile she had no covenant promises of provision. And apparently, she had no one in this world to turn to either.

She was gathering sticks to make a fire to bake the little loaf when Elijah the prophet, hungry, thirsty, and tired from fleeing wicked King Ahab of Israel, walked up to the gate of her city and observed her searching for firewood. God had told Elijah that He already had spoken to the woman to feed him until the famine ended. Emboldened with this knowledge, Elijah frankly asked her for some water. He called to her, "Fetch me, I pray thee, a little water in a vessel, that I may drink."

Perhaps she recognized that he was a prophet, for without delay she stopped her search for firewood and turned to fetch him a drink. But then Elijah decided to test the word he'd heard from the Lord earlier, for as she went for the water, he called to her again:

"Bring me, I pray thee, a morsel of bread in thine hand."

The woman froze. She wanted to be hospitable; it was the customary thing to do. But her son's need came first. She may have not been a woman of faith, but she was a woman of honesty. Instead of claiming she had nothing to give, she spoke the truth:

As the Lord thy God liveth, I have not a cake, but a handful of meal in a barrel, and a little oil in a cruise: and, behold, I am gathering two sticks, that I may go in and dress it for me and my son, that we may eat it, and die. I Kings 17:12

Note that she referred to Jehovah as "thy" God, meaning Elijah's God, not hers. She also said she and her son would eat one more meal and die. So there should be no doubt in your mind as to where this woman's faith was: it wasn't in God but in the evil facts of her circumstances, which fairly shouted imminent death. Then Elijah said to her:

Fear not; go and do as thou hast said: but make me

thereof a little cake first, and bring it unto me, and after make for thee and thy son.

For thus saith the Lord God of Israel, The barrel of meal shall not waste, neither shall the cruse of oil fail, until the day that the Lord sendeth rain upon the earth. I Kings 17:13–14

Verses 15–16 record what happened next. Having nothing to lose—she and her son were going to die anyway—the woman took a chance on the word of God. She used the little bit of flour and oil she had left to make a loaf for Elijah and served it to him. But after doing so, when she returned to the flour barrel and the oil keg, miraculously they had filled up again, as they did day after day until the famine ended. Elijah lived with the widow for one year, and just as God had said, daily He sent the widow miracle flour and oil, enough to feed Elijah, the widow, and her son for the remainder of the famine.

The word famine does not appear in I King 17, the chapter that tells the story of the miracle flour and oil. It does say, however, that there would be no rain for several years (verse 1). Regardless, Jesus confirmed that drought conditions had led to a grievous famine during the time when the widow fed Elijah:

But I tell you of a truth, many widows were in Israel in the days of Elijah, when the heaven was shut up three years and six months, when great famine was throughout all the land;

But unto none of them was Elijah sent, save unto Sarepta, a city of Sidon, unto a woman that was a widow. Luke 4:25–26

I've included all of Jesus' reference to the Gentile widow because there's more in these two verses than just confirmation of famine. Jesus singled her out for her faith. Yet at first glance it appears the widow didn't have any, or at least not enough to bring her to Jesus' attention. Consider: 1) She called Jehovah "thy" God, not "my" God; 2) by her own mouth she spoke what she believed would happen: she was waiting for herself and her son to die—hardly words of faith—even though God had already spoken to her that they would live.

If that's not enough evidence of the widow's unbelief in God's goodness and provision, there is another episode in this chapter that reveals the fullness of her doubt.

And it came to pass after these things, that the son of the woman, the mistress of the house, fell sick; and his sickness was so sore, that there was no breath left in him.

And she said unto Elijah, What have I to do with thee, O thou man of God? art thou come unto me to call my sin to remembrance, and to slay my son? I Kings 17:17–18

Following this accusation of the prophet and acknowledgment of her sin, the widow turned her dead son over to Elijah, who carried him up to the loft of the house to his (Elijah's) own bed. He prayed for the child three times, his soul returned to his body, and the prophet happily returned the resurrected child to his mother.

But listen to her profession of faith, the first

positive words we hear from her mouth: "Now by this I know that thou art a man of God, and that the word of the Lord is in thy mouth is truth." (I Kings 17:24) It took the resurrection of her child from the dead for this widow to finally believe the anointing on Elijah's life; deliverance from famine wasn't enough for her. Because she was not a Jew, she hadn't benefited from hearing the promises in the law or the accounts of Jewish ancestors who had been delivered from the Egyptian's sword or fed miracle bread and water in the desert. All she had known until now was tragedy and lack. It was not easy for her to believe in God's goodness.

Witness the marvel of faith. This woman had no blood covenant with God, was not a descendant of Abraham therefore could not claim Abraham's blessings, her confession was marked by doubt, and she deserved no good thing from the Lord. God had spoken to her that she would feed a prophet, herself, and her son, but when the prophet arrived on her doorstep asking to be fed, at first she ignored God's promise, claiming she and her son would die of starvation brought on by famine, a confession of unbelief and death.

Yet God delivered her from famine!

Jesus pointed out in his sermon at the Nazarene synagogue (Luke 4:17–27) that there were many Jewish widows at the time of this famine. God could have sent Elijah to any of them, but He sent him to this particular widow, a pagan. There was no outward difference between the Gentile and the Israelite widows. All were suffering the grievous effects of drought and the hunger that followed. But there was an inward difference between this widow and the others, and that difference was faith. Hers was very small faith indeed: after all, how much faith does it take to give away your last swallow of food when you've already resigned yourself to death by starvation? Even you have more faith than that. But when she acted on God's word and fed the prophet, she acted in faith, and God was watching.

If this undeserving woman—who was outside the covenant of Abraham, who knew little of the goodness and merciful character of the Israelite God, who still doubted after the first miracle and was unbelieving until the end—could get delivered from famine, why can't you? What stops you from believing the testimony concerning God's deliverance in the Book of Haggai? What stops you from acting on his promise to restore what you've lost found in the Book of Joel? He delivered David and all Israel from three years of famine, and we know how stubborn, unbelieving, and disobedient the Israelite nation was. God reclaimed the land and seven years of harvests for the Shunammite woman. He rebuilt the house of Elimelech after death had taken his childless sons, extending his grace with such magnitude and absolute forgiveness as to make his widow Naomi the great-great grandmother of King David.

How little God requires. All this Gentile widow did was take one baby step of faith. She believed God's word and gave. Her little loaf of bread, in its preciousness to her, was no different than what Joel proclaimed was needed for a miracle for the Israelites, a blessing, "even a meat offering and a drink offering unto the Lord your God"—which is what her gift of the bread and oil to the prophet, God's messenger, became:

an offering to God. What God did for the widow when He sent Elijah to her was to give her an opportunity to put God first. Likely she took that step of faith with her last mouthful of food because Elijah's prophecy regarding the barrel of flour and keg of oil was the same word God had already spoken to her heart before Elijah arrived in Sarepta. When God is about to do something He confirms his word by repeating Himself. (Genesis 41:32)

With that thought in mind, let's look at one more person who got God's attention by a simple offering made in faith.

9. The Lesson of Noah

What Noah experienced after the flood was not a
classic famine as we think of famine, yet God
specifically used this word when he named Noah in
Ezekiel 14:12–14 as an example of how he saves the
righteous when He sends famine. The devastation
wreaked by the flooding of the whole earth had the
same ruinous effect as famine that occurs in a select
area, but the flood in Noah's time was worse because of
its totality. God didn't just wipe out all the food in the
earth, He wiped out every living thing, plant and
animal, as well. In a classic (natural) famine limited to a
geographical area, you always have the option of
pulling up stakes, as the Shunammite woman and
Elimelech did, relocating temporarily wherever you can
find food until the famine ends. But Noah did not have
this option. The flood covered the entire earth. There
was nowhere for Noah to go to wait it out but inside the
ark.

God sent this first recorded flood because of sin,
which was so egregious in Noah's time that God

regretted He had ever made man and woman:

And God saw that the wickedness of man was great in the earth, and that every imagination of the thoughts of his heart was only evil continually.
And it repented the Lord that he had made man on the earth, and it grieved him at this heart.
Genesis 6:5–6

God was compelled to act:

And the Lord said, I will destroy man whom I have created from the face of the earth; both man, and beast, and the creeping thing, and the fowls of the air; for it repenteth me that I have made them. Genesis 6:7

You know what happened next. God told Noah to build the ark, he and his family and male/female pairs of all living things (except water creatures, of course) entered the ark, it began to rain and continued raining forty days and nights, the whole earth flooded, and all creatures perished except for those inside the ark and those in the water. Finally the water dried up, the ark came to rest on the mountains of Ararat (extreme eastern Turkey near the border with Iran), and Noah waited to see what God would have him do next.

What is relevant here is God's response to Noah's actions when he finally stepped onto dry ground:

And Noah builded an altar unto the Lord; and took of every clean beast, and of every clean fowl, and offered burnt offerings on the altar.
And the Lord smelled a sweet savour; and the Lord

*said in his heart, I will not again curse the ground any
more for man's sake; for the imagination of man's
heart is evil from his youth; neither will I again smite
any more every thing living, as I have done.*

*While the earth remaineth, seedtime and harvest,
and cold and heat, and summer and winter, and day
and night shall not cease.* Genesis 8:20–22

So what was it about Noah's sacrifice that so
moved God? Noah's practice of making sacrificial
offerings was not new. He had made them before the
flood; the practice had been handed down for
generations. The Bible records that as far back as Cain
and Abel—the first children born to Adam and Eve—
people brought offerings to God, presumably to be
sacrificed on some sort of altar. Because Noah
sacrificed animals to God after the flood, surely he
sacrificed them before the flood. To make sure there
was a supply of sacrifices after the flood, God told
Noah to take along seven pairs each of (ceremonially)
clean animals. You'll remember from Sunday school
that God commanded Noah to take with him single
pairs of animals, but these were only unclean beasts,
those not used in sacrifice. (Genesis 7:2) So if God
expected Noah to offer sacrifices after the flood as He
had before the flood, why was this particular sacrifice
so special to God, so special that the Holy Spirit made a
point of recording God's contented response? What was
it about this particular sacrifice that moved the heart of
God?

The answer is not in the *what* of Noah's sacrifice
but in the *when.* At this point in the biblical account,
Noah was sacrificing the usual clean animals, but never

before this moment was he called to do so by faith alone. Remember that God told Noah it was going to rain forty days and nights (Genesis 7:4), and He also told him to prepare food for all who entered the ark. So Noah crammed the ark with as much food as he thought it would take to keep all within alive for forty days and some undisclosed period thereafter, but Noah and his family spent a lot longer than forty days in the ark. Genesis 7:24 says the waters remained on the earth five months and that Noah did not leave the ark until the ground was dry. (Genesis 8:13) By that time, the food supply remaining in the ark must have been severely reduced.

And what did Noah see when he stepped out of the dimness of his watery house into the glare of daylight after all those months? Utter devastation and ruin. Every grain and vegetable field, all trees, all natural vegetation, all wild game—every food source had been swept away. For Noah and his family, their food for many months until their first harvest would be only what was left in the ark, fish they could catch, and whatever edible plants they could forage from the tender growth beginning to sprout around them.

Noah had several big, immediate problems on his hands. His first obligation was to God, to see that the supply of sacrificial animals was not inadvertently consumed so that there would always be offerings on God's altar. His second obligation was to his family, to ensure that they had enough to eat. His third obligation was to see that the last male/female pair of every creature was likewise not consumed, to ensure that their line would continue. Just like you, Noah was forced to set priorities from his limited natural supply. And just as it is for you, for Noah this was a crucial test of his faith in the integrity of God and his word.

Would God feed them? Could God's promise to care for him and his family be trusted? Would God restore the earth to its former abundance, fully voiding the effects of famine caused by the flood? Noah had God's quiet word from before the flood, but he also had something that screamed at him every day after the flood: utter devastation and ruin everywhere he looked. A dwindling, uncertain food supply. A hungry family.

Like the Gentile widow, Noah looked hunger in the face ... and ignored it. He denied the power of impending starvation by taking the most precious thing he had, a portion of his family's dwindling food supply, and offered it to God in sacrificial worship. Noah's act of faith, just like the Gentile widow's, was actually a statement sent heavenward: "I believe, Lord, that you will provide for me and my family." And as in the case of the Gentile widow, it was Noah's singular act of faith that caught God's attention and moved Him in his heart. Essentially Noah affirmed to God, himself, and his family that God and not the food in the ark was his real source of supply. His simple act of worship was the best leadership he could demonstrate to encourage the little band of survivors that they were going to be okay.

Noah's worship was also his ultimate statement of faith in God's integrity, in his goodness. Because though it is true that Noah and his family were spared the destruction of the punishing rains, and so his offering expressed worship and thanksgiving, it is also true that not spared were his home and the comforts thereof; his village and customary means of support for himself and his family; his relatives, friends, and neighbors—all of life as he knew it. Noah could have dwelled on what he had lost and lost through no fault of his own. Genesis 6:8–9 says that Noah found favor with God because he "was a just man and perfect in his generations," and that he "walked with God." Noah is another example of one of God's people who saw famine in his time though he wasn't guilty of anything that would provoke God to such extreme.

Knowing this, Noah could have become offended at God's terrible display of righteous anger. He could have questioned God's judgment upon surveying the overwhelming obliteration of God's rebellious people, the awful roar of justice exercised by an all-powerful God who had pitted Himself against impotent, puny, insignificant creation, humans and animals alike. But instead, in a testament to God's goodness, Noah gave thanks that his near kin was spared, and He worshipped God for who He is. By doing so Noah acknowledged his powerlessness in the presence of and submission to God. In the wake of the most complete destruction, death, and loss the planet had ever experienced, Noah's worship was his testimony to the world that, no matter what, God is God, and God is good.

Though it was too late for those who perished, Noah's act of devotion in the face of famine purchased for posterity a precious promise from God, because Noah's sacrifice of something vitally dear to him touched God's heart. The Bible says that's where—in his heart, not his head—God determined to never again afflict creation in similar manner. *Noah's faith, expressed through an offering, moved God's heart,* thereby purchasing for his descendants a promise that never again would the entire earth be devastated by flood waters.

Of his own accord God affirmed his promise by setting a "bow" or rainbow in the sky.

And God said, This is the token of the covenant which I make between me and you and every living creature that is with you, for perpetual generations:

I do set my bow in the cloud, and it shall be for a token of a covenant between me and the earth.

And it shall come to pass, when I bring a cloud over the earth, that the bow shall be seen in the cloud:

And I will remember my covenant, which is between me and you and every living creature of all flesh; and the waters shall no more become a flood to destroy all flesh.

And the bow shall be in the cloud; and I will look upon it, that I may remember the everlasting covenant between God and every living creature of all flesh that is upon the earth. Genesis 9:12–16

It's noteworthy that God says in verse 16 that He will look upon the rainbow as a reminder to *Himself* of his covenant with the earth. If God prepares reminders for Himself, ought not we to do the same? The rainbow is a reminder to us also of God's covenant, but there is more.

As long as the earth remains, the rainbow reminds us of a special man, his special offering, and how giving that which is most precious to us gets God's attention. An offering from our heart touches his heart and contains within itself the spiritual power to move the hand of God. When we see a rainbow we are reminded that, better than any words can speak, a sacrificial, heartfelt offering is a powerful expression of our faith and trust in God in the midst of our terrible circumstances, even famine.

I speak from experience. Several years ago I set my own rainbow of faith into the dark cloud that hung over my home. Around 1995, while still bracing the winds of a howling financial famine, when my family and I were still renting after losing our house and I was still unemployed (except for occasional freelance work that was never enough to make a dent in our financial circumstances), during that awful time someone handed me a book filled with pure gold. *Moving the Hand of God: Putting Memorial Prayer to Work for You* by John Avanzini[1] opened my eyes to the power of the sacrificial offering. I read that book in about one hour, and as soon as I was finished, I put it down on the couch, stood up in the middle of my living room, and right then told God I was going to make a sacrificial offering. I told him I expected Him to receive it according to his word and that I was expecting a MIRACLE in my finances in return. In fact, my faith was so strong after reading that powerful book, that I told God I wasn't expecting ordinary increase. A promotion or raise for my husband was not what I was looking for. A job for me wasn't it either. These would be nice, I told God, but they wouldn't be a MIRACLE. I wanted the hand of God to reach into the midst of my famine. I wanted something *supernatural*, and told Him

---

[1] Harrison House: Tulsa, OK, 1990. Reprinted as *Breakthrough for Unanswered Prayer,* HIS Publishing Company, Tulsa, OK, 1993.

so.

But I had no money whatsoever to make an offering, only debts. The only thing of value I could think to sell to raise cash to give as an offering was our old, beat-up, 1936 upright piano. It had a key that even the repairman couldn't fix, and the dilapidated housing looked terrible. But I figured another family, less affluent than us (there's always someone worse off than you) would embrace it for cheap music lessons just as we had done a few years earlier. I ran an ad and sold it for around $200 and immediately planted it in Christian ministry.

Then I waited. But I didn't wait passively. Regularly, nearly every day, I thanked God for my supernatural financial miracle, and I always reminded Him that I was expecting a MIRACLE, something to break the back of famine that had come to ravage my home. I told my kids that God was going to give us a house! (I said it just like that, with a big, bright smile on my face: "God is going to give us a house!") They would sit on our battered old couch, eyes filled with suspicion, saying nothing, but I knew what they were thinking. *Mom is going off again. Better not to say anything to encourage her. Maybe if we don't respond she'll shut up.*

But I was not deterred, because finally I had a rainbow. I'd look in the corner of the living room and see my rainbow, a big blank space where the piano had been. That blank space reminded me daily that I had made a sacrificial offering, God had received it, and I had a miracle coming! And you know, just because it was an old, beat-up piano didn't mean it was not an offering of value. It was an ugly old piano, but it was

71

the only piano I could afford, and selling it meant I no longer had an instrument on which my children could practice. I didn't like that thought (they loved it) but there was something I wanted so much more than piano lessons for my kids. I wanted to see God move again in our lives. And now I had the faith to make it happen.

I've already told you that, two years later, God gave us a mortgage-free house, which definitely was my supernatural move of the hand of God in our circumstances. It was my miracle. Prior to receiving the new house, I had been only limping along in my faith, hoping for an affordable mortgage. That didn't take much faith: it's the American way to believe God for more debt. But not once during my two-year period of believing, confessing, and thanking God for a miracle did it enter my head that God would give us a fully-paid-for home. But God knew that if we had a mortgage-free home, then the money we needed to get out of debt would automatically be in our hands. Because if you don't have a mortgage, you have lots more cash to pay off your debts. So in one move of the hand of God, the effects of the famine were undone.

God truly restored to me and my family the years that the locust had eaten. And what he did for us, He'll do for you.

10. David's Sin, David's Sacrifice

David faced famine a second time during his reign, but the second instance had a sadder ending than the first. II Samuel 24 tells the story, which closes with an important lesson if you want to end the famine in your life.

For reasons not disclosed, God was angry at Israel and moved David to take a head count of all men fit to fight. Probably God sought an opportunity to slay Israel—it wouldn't have been the first time. David's military general, Joab, advised David not to number the soldiers, but David insisted and ten months later, Joab reported back to David with the head count for Israel and Judah. Soon afterward David realized he had sinned in numbering his soldiers, because he trusted in his army instead of God to win his country's battles. He prayed, repented, and asked God to take away his sin. The next morning Gad, David's "seer" or prophet, paid him a visit.

Thus saith the Lord, I offer thee three things;

73

choose thee one of them, that I may do it unto thee ...
Shall seven years of famine come unto thee in thy
land? or wilt thou flee three months before thine
enemies, while they pursue thee? or that there be three
days' pestilence in thy land? now advise, and see what
answer I shall return to him that sent me. II Samuel
24:12–13

David answered: "I am in a great strait: let us fall
now into the hand of the Lord; for his mercies are great:
and let me not fall into the hand of man." (II Samuel
24:14) At David's request, instead of war or famine
God sent three days of pestilence, which killed seventy
thousand men before God stopped the plague.

David had to choose among three evils, three
punishments sent by God to administer a deadly justice
designed to lead to repentance. Three days of
pestilence, David surmised, would simply take less time
to do it. Seven years of famine would be long and
torturous. Three months of attacks by Israel's enemies
was unthinkable. David could not bear to have his
people fall into the hands of sword-wielding,
bloodthirsty Gentiles. So that left the only tolerable
alternative: three days wherein Israel would be pursued
by the angel of the Lord (evidenced in this
circumstance as pestilence), because, David knew, it is
better to deal with an angry but merciful God than any
earthly enemy. David did not choose famine, but he
chose a punishment that, from the context of the story,
was just as destructive. Weighed together, pestilence,
enemy attacks, and famine were different but equally
effective methods for God to achieve the same sad
result.

God grieved at the death of so many of his people and so did David. When he saw the angel of the Lord at the threshing floor of Araunah, he prayed: "Lo, I have sinned, and I have done wickedly: but these sheep, what have they done? let thine hand, I pray thee, be against me, and against my father's house." (II Samuel 24:17) Moved by David's selfless prayer, God desired to restore Israel, so He sent Gad to tell David to set up an altar to offer sacrifices at the threshing floor. When Araunah saw David and his men coming toward his property, he ran to meet them, bowing himself with his face to the ground. David told Araunah why he had come, and at once the landowner insisted on giving David all the animals he needed to sacrifice. He even offered David the wooden tools from his threshing floor, including the yoke for the oxen, to provide fuel for the altar fire. But David refused to offer on the altar anything he had received as a gift:

I will surely buy it of thee at a price: neither will I offer burnt offerings unto the Lord my God of that which doth cost me nothing. So David bought the threshing floor and the oxen for fifty shekels of silver.
And David built there an altar unto the Lord, and offered burnt offerings. So the Lord was entreated for the land, and the plague was stayed from Israel.
II Samuel 24–25

Here we see that old-fashioned word again, *entreated.* It's no coincidence that God was entreated for the land and the plague was stopped following the same order of events for which He was entreated and the land healed when David first saw famine as king of

Israel. First there was disobedience, then there was punishment, then God's people made sacrifices, then God brought restoration. We see this pattern repeatedly in the Bible, because this is the pattern to end famine and instigate restoration. The evidence is plain:

- God told David to set up an altar for sacrifice after he prayed for God to end the slaughter of the Israelites.
- Joel told the priests to fast and pray, hoping that God would provide what they needed for a meat and drink offering.
- The prodigal son returned to his father prepared to make a sacrifice of himself.
- The widow of Sarepta gave her last meal.
- Noah gave from his dwindling food supply.
- Even David's first experience with famine demanded a sacrifice to bring an end to it: Saul's seven sons were hanged before God turned away his anger and healed the land. (Don't interpret this as human sacrifice, which God condemns. The death of Saul's sons was justice for the Gibeonites, not atonement for Saul's sin.)

David understood the connection between famine and sacrifice, but just as important, he knew that an offering that cost him nothing was no offering at all. He had to put something of himself into the sacrifice, so he insisted on paying Araunah what was reasonable for the oxen and the use of his threshing floor. Jesus paid the ultimate and final blood sacrifice for us, of course, so God is no longer impressed with the fragrance of smoking animal fat. But what hasn't changed is that, as with all the people chronicled here who suffered a famine sent by God, He's still looking for a sacrifice that represents *you*, and He knows whether your offering costs you anything.

Considering all you've been through and all you've learned, my question to you is: What are you willing to sacrifice to bring an end to the famine in your life?

11. Your Hiding Place

I rejoiced when God spoke to me through II Kings 8, the story of the Shunammite woman whose house and land were restored after seven years of famine. He was telling me that He had plans to restore my house and finances. I also learned a few other things about famine by studying that chapter, things I will share with you shortly. But there was something about this passage that troubled me. The entire story is recorded in just six verses, so let's take a look at them.

Then spake Elisha unto the woman, whose son he had restored to life, saying, Arise, and go thou and thine household, and sojourn wheresoever thou canst sojourn: for the Lord hath called for a famine; and it shall also come upon the land seven years.

And the woman arose, and did after the saying of the man of God: and she went with her household, and sojourned in the land of the Philistines seven years.

And it came to pass at the seven years' end, that

*the woman returned out of the land of the Philistines:
and she went forth to cry unto the king for her house
and for her land.*

*And the king talked with Gehazi the servant of the
man of God, saying, Tell me, I pray thee, all the great
things that Elisha hath done.*

*And it came to pass, as he was telling the king how
he had restored a dead body to life, that, behold, the
woman, whose son he had restored to life, cried to the
king for her house and for her land. And Gehazi said,
My lord, O king, this is the woman, and this is her son,
whom Elisha restored to life.*

*And when the king asked the woman, she told him.
So the king appointed unto her a certain officer, saying,
Restore all that was hers, and all the fruits of the field
since the day that she left the land, even until now.*
II Kings 8:1–6

One thing about my family's situation that I
already knew because God had told me was that, like
the famine recorded here, the famine we were
experiencing had been ordered by Him. This may be
hard for you to receive, but it wasn't for me. It
encouraged me, because when God told me famine had
come to our home, finally I knew that what I had
suspected all along was true: my family's evil
circumstances were under God's control and that
through them He meant to do something good in our
lives. I was honored that God had shared this
knowledge with me, and I was grateful because finally I
knew how to pray for an end to our awful situation. I
knew, too, that God was sharing revelation with me that
few others had. I am still waiting to hear a sermon

about famine.

I also knew that because God had called the famine, it would not last longer than seven years. No record exists of a biblical famine extending beyond this God-ordained period. This is so because it is not God's intention to destroy you, just correct you, (but you will *feel* like you're being destroyed), to complete a work in you He started when you were born again. The most frequently cited number in the Bible, seven represents spiritual completion or perfection, either for good or evil.[2] When God offered David his choice of three punishments after he numbered his soldiers, if David chose famine, God said, it would last seven years. Joseph told Pharaoh that the famine in Egypt would last seven years and that God had ordained it. (Genesis 41:30–32) The punishment God sent to Israel at the hand of the Midianites, who robbed them of all their sustenance during Gideon's time, lasted seven years. (Judges 6:6) And here in II Kings 8 we plainly see the hand of God behind this seven-year famine.

On March 13, 1991, I walked away from my editor job in Birmingham, Alabama to follow my husband's job transfer to Washington, D.C. Sometime after the troubles began, when God spoke to me that He had called for a famine on our house, I quickly calculated that it might be Spring 1998 before I held a good job again, because the lack of well-paying work in my field was the chief factor contributing to our financial problems; the house that wouldn't sell was a big factor

---

[2] Robert D. Johnston. *Numbers in the Bible*. Kregel Publications, Grand Rapids, MI, 1990. p. 71.

too, but a secondary one. I told a Christian counselor during this period that I was so convinced that God had sent famine to our house that I believed that, although I might not obtain a good job *before* March 13, 1998 (even after I'd applied for several hundred jobs), I certainly would obtain it no *later* than that date. God would not deny his word. Our famine would not extend beyond March 13, 1998. I told the counselor that if I didn't have a job before March 13, then I absolutely, unfailingly believed the phone would ring *on* that date and my employment famine would be over.

Indeed, on March 13, 1998 the phone rang. It was a Christian ministry calling to interview me for a job. Within a week I was earning again.

Finally, I learned from II Kings 8 that when the famine on our home ended, God would assign to me, like he had to the Shunammite woman, someone to retrieve what the locust had taken from me. The king appointed an officer to ensure she got her land and seven years of harvests back. God would do the same for me, and I told Him so, over and over again, confessing this word to Him while I waited for the famine to end and the restoration to begin.

But, like I said, despite all the encouragement I gleaned from this story, I was still troubled. The Shunammite woman and her family had a place to get their needs met while they waited for the famine to end, but I didn't. I wasn't free to pack up my household and leave, because the famine was on my household. If we moved it moved with us. In addition, God had not told me to build an ark to preserve us like He had told Noah; and besides, rain wasn't our problem. So what refuge did God have for me? How was I to get my basic needs met, and that of my family, while I waited for God to finish the work of famine in our home that He had started?

God answered these questions in a quiet but profound way one day when I was at home alone. I had been struggling for several days, frankly wondering at God's justice. So many of my circumstances were beyond my control, just as in the case of the Shunammite woman. *But He rescued her! He gave her a way of escape. He told her exactly what to do and where to go.* All God had told me was that He was behind the famine we were experiencing. *Now what?* I thought. *How can I overcome the unbelief, the evil circumstances, the lack and destruction I see all around me?* I felt powerless. It's impossible to oppose God and win. Why try?

I was thinking these gloomy thoughts as I got up from a chair in the kitchen. As I stepped into the living room God spoke loudly into my spirit.

"YOUR FAITH IS STRONGER THAN ANYONE'S UNBELIEF."

In an instant, God revealed to me the hiding place He had prepared for me: my faith. He showed me the nature of faith, that it is more powerful than anyone's unbelief, no matter how much influence that person has over your life, no matter how close that person is to you. If I would use my faith during this period of famine, God would meet my needs.

I had plenty of opportunities to test his promise.

One fall I was looking down the road toward Christmas, knowing that we didn't have money for gifts for our four children (we had the fourth child after we moved to Virginia). I appealed to God for some kind of work, even if it wasn't editorial work, which I had been doing before the famine rolled over our lives. I managed to find a one-time, at-home proofreading job. I worked long, tiring hours on that manuscript, reading highly technical pages, and finally, with dollar signs dancing in my head instead of sugar plums, I submitted it to my client. A thousand dollars they were going to pay me! That would well take care of the kids' Christmas. I was so happy and thankful to be able to do something to bring in some money for gifts for my children.

I waited impatiently through early December for the check, but it didn't arrive. Finally I called and was told that it would be late January before they could send payment—more than a month away. I couldn't wait that long, but not knowing what to say, I thanked them and hung up the phone.

What should I do? I stewed a while. Then it occurred to me that this check was the money I had believed for, the money God had sent to provide for my children's Christmas presents. It was already mine and *it was on time*, no matter what the client said, *because God is never late.* I was just going to have to insist in the spirit realm that I get my money—I'd done the work and it was legally owed to me—but it was more than that. Now my faith was talking to me, and it was saying GO GET WHAT GOD HAS PROVIDED FOR YOU. IT'S ALREADY YOURS. DON'T ACCEPT NO.

After a few days of building up my faith, I called the client back.

"Hello, this is Virginia Welch, the proofreader you hired. You had said you couldn't pay my proofreading bill until the end of next month. Well, you know (gulp,

gulp) the only reason I took this job is to pay for Christmas presents for my four children. Do you think it's possible that you could talk to your accounting department and have them print a check right away? I'd really appreciate it. Thank you."

Later that afternoon the phone rang and the client was on the other end. They were mailing me a check immediately.

From the day that God spoke to me about using my faith as a hiding place, the whole famine situation changed for me. In one word God dispelled the depression and hopelessness that had clouded my mind for several years. I no longer felt that I was powerless to do anything about our circumstances (now there's a mindset that will lead to depression). I had my faith! There was something I could *do* to bring change. My faith, I learned, was like money in my hand to spend as I wished. I could buy whatever I needed with this gold coin, this marvelous, precious substance that got me what I needed from Heaven.

The revelation that faith was my hiding place confirmed to me two things. One, God is no "respecter" of persons (Acts 10:34), meaning, He isn't impressed with anyone's title, ancestry, position, or whatever else impresses people. He is impressed by and responds to faith, and what He's done for others He'll do for you, if you'll believe Him to do it. He provided a hiding place for the Shunammite woman during famine; He provided one for me; therefore, if you must wait a while for Him to complete a work in your home, you can pray and believe that He'll provide a hiding place for you. By hiding place I mean a very real, tangible place of provision. It's where you get your basic needs met until the famine is over. It's not your need that moves the hand of God. If that were true the whole world would have full stomachs and be clothed and healed. It's your faith in God that attracts his resources to your need.

The second revelation: God's word is the complete instruction manual for living. The Holy Spirit recorded the stories of the Old Testament to train you in righteousness. (II Timothy 3:16) You can read about biblical famines and apply the wisdom you find in each story to your own situation. I love the way the Bible reads on this score: "For whatsoever things were written aforetime were written for our learning, that we through patience and comfort of the scriptures might have hope." Romans 15:4

12. What You Must Do

You're convinced that famine has come to your house. You see yourself in these pages and know the book you hold in your hands is no accident; God sent it to you. *Finally*, you think to yourself, *someone understands what I'm going through.* You're beginning to make sense of the calamities that have befallen you as you realize that God is in the midst of your awful circumstances. After reading the accounts of others who suffered a famine sent by God, you have concluded that, for you, God and his way of deliverance is your way out of your present pain.

You are right. He is your deliverance. But there are still some things you must do to see Him work that deliverance into your situation. Just as He is responsible to bring you out of where He has brought you in, you have responsibilities to do things his way as He directs, and I wouldn't disappoint you by not spelling them out plainly. We've looked at what others did to turn famine away, but let's bring their actions into modern terms so you can apply the wisdom of the scriptures to your personal situation. I've had to walk every one of the steps listed here, and I assure you they work.

1) *Ask God why.* "The curse causeless shall not come." (Proverbs 26:2) There's a reason for everything that happens to you as a Christian, even if it isn't readily apparent, and even if it's not God's will. David was fearless in asking God why a famine had come to Israel; you be fearless too. God will answer you swiftly and speak in a way you can understand. When I asked God why famine had come to our house He spoke to me in less than two hours. He wants you to know why you're suffering so you can do something about it.

2) *Repent if necessary.* If you need to repent of some sin, and you inquire of God what that might be, He will be quick to tell you this too. He wants you to correct your ways even more than you want to change (that's why he sent you famine!). If you haven't sinned but know that your spouse is outside God's will and your house has suffered famine as a result, pray that God sends conviction and convinces him or her of the need to repent. And pray that God helps you to forgive your spouse from your heart. Learning to forgive may be the chief lesson you are meant to learn through your ordeal.

3) *Fast.* In spiritual warfare, famine is not a skirmish, a military dust-up that calls for light arms. It's a bloody battle between spiritual titans (you and Satan) that requires bigger fire power than ordinary prayer. In Joel chapters 1 and 2, Joel told the priests and all the people to fast to bring God's restoration into their circumstances. When God wanted to restore a home to my family after we'd lost ours, He told me to fast also.

Famine is heavy spiritual bondage. It takes more than just prayer to break it.

I had to fast once a week for months before God told me I had fasted enough. I may have fasted weekly the entire two years, 1993 to 1995, though I no longer remember exactly how long God required me to keep this up. (I do remember that I fell away from the habit during one holiday season. Christmas came and went, January arrived, and I was still dragging my feet about returning to weekly fasting. God gently reminded me that the holidays were past and I had no more excuse. Promptly I returned to a weekly fast.) While fasting I had to "cry unto the king for my house and for my land," just as the Shunammite woman did when she returned from the land of the Philistines after seven years of famine and found that squatters had taken over her property. (II Kings 8:5) Satan is the squatter who has moved into your home. You shouldn't be surprised, then, if you must use spiritual weapons of prayer and fasting to evict him. Fasting is never pleasant, but I can say that when I was obedient, God's grace was with me in a tangible way. It was far easier for me to go without food on these fasts that He directed than it had been in the past when I had fasted on my own.

4) *Put God's work first.* Here is the heart and soul of Haggai's message: God first. It doesn't matter what you must do to make it reality in your life, you must put God first or you will not be blessed. First in your time, first in your finances, first in your thought life, first in your aspirations. God first is the only way. Make the commitment right now to make Him first and you will have made the most concrete step possible toward a life of blessing.

5) *Give offerings.* Give what is precious. Give regularly. Read the Book of Haggai over and over again until his words about the importance of offerings sink in deep. You can make no greater statement of faith in God's ability to sustain you than to give to Him something that is in short supply. This is what Noah did and as you saw, it moved God's heart.

Some Christians today argue that sacrificial offering of material wealth at the Lord's altar is no longer necessary, because Jesus made the full and final sacrifice for our sin, but their logic is faulty. It is true that we cannot give anything to God to purchase our salvation—that's why God, in the person of Jesus, came to give Himself as a sacrifice on our behalf. But the practice of giving offerings has nothing to do with our salvation. It is an entirely separate topic.

What I speak of here is a sacrificial act of giving that demonstrates the seriousness of the heart. Much like fasting, which is another form of sacrifice, a material offering is a tangible demonstration to God of our sincerity and fervency. Throughout the Old and New Testaments God's people are urged to give sacrificially. References to offering(s) appear more than 1,100 times in the Bible; references to sacrifice(s) appear 360 times; references to gift(s) occur more than 100 times; and references to vow(s) (often made in the form of material gifts) occur about 80 times. Truly, God is interested in the gifts we bring to Him.

What's more, gifts given from a pure heart, given with a pure motive, gifts that cost us, get his attention. Consider Hannah, wife of Elkanah the Ephrathite. In 1 Samuel 1 we read of this childless woman who grieved at her barren state while she prayed year after year to

conceive. Finally, in desperation she vowed to the Lord
to dedicate any child born to her to his service.

*In her deep anguish Hannah prayed to the LORD,
weeping bitterly. And she made a vow, saying, "Lord
Almighty, if you will only look on your servant's misery
and remember me, and not forget your servant but give
her a son, then I will give him to the Lord for all the
days of his life, and no razor will ever be used on his
head.* 1 Samuel 1:1–11

In due time Hannah conceived and bore Samuel,
who became a great priest and prophet in Israel. His
birth was followed by the birth of five siblings. But
make note: She did not conceive until she vowed to
give to God the first child He gave her.

There was also Cornelius, whose offerings (alms)
were, according to Acts 10, a memorial before God.
*Cornelius' giving caused thoughts of him and his
petitions to be continually in God's mind.* Read what
the Bible says about this nonbeliever:

*There was a certain man in Caesarea called
Cornelius, a centurion of the band called the Italian
band,*

*A devout man, and one that feared God with all his
house, which gave much alms to the people, and prayed
to God alway.*

*He saw in a vision evidently about the ninth hour
of the day an angel of God coming in to him, and
saying unto him, Cornelius.*

*And when he looked on him, he was afraid, and
said, What is it, Lord? And he said unto him, Thy*

prayers and thine alms are come up for a memorial before God. Acts 10:1-4

Contrary to what the naysayers believe, God does take a keen interest in our giving: what we give and how we give. Forty-one times in the Old Testament God instructed the Jews that their animal sacrifices must be "without blemish," meaning God expected them to give sacrificially, the best that they had—no injured, sick, or weak animal makes a sacrifice fit for a king. In the New Testament God instructs us to give cheerfully (2 Corinthians 9:7) and weekly (1 Corinthians 16:2). Paul praised the saints at Jerusalem who, from their "deep poverty" gave liberally of their material goods to meet the needs of Christians worse off than they. (2 Corinthians 8) Surely, if our Lord took note of the widow's mite (Mark 12:42–44) and what it cost her to cast it into the offering box, He is watching us also to see if what we give to his service costs us.

The money I gave to God's work from the sale of my children's piano was, like Cornelius' alms, a memorial for me, and that's how I thought of it while I waited for God to act on my behalf. It was a continual reminder to me and to Him that I was waiting for Him to do a miracle for me, something so big and so good that the years of famine would be forgotten. I urge you to create your own memorial while you wait on God to deliver you from the ravages of famine.

6) *Confess and expect.* Make sure your mouth lines up with God's word. *Expect* God to break the famine off your household and *confess* what good things He is doing for you toward that end. Confess that you have (right now!) what you're believing for. It is scriptural to

do this (Mark 11:23; Romans 10:10; II Corinthians 4:13), and as a bonus, your faith will grow as your ears hear your lips speaking words of faith. And when you confess what you believe He's doing, thank Him for doing it.

7) *Walk by faith.* Faith is a decision. If God must work a little longer in your spouse's life or yours, if you must wait a while to see the famine end as I did, decide that you will believe God's word to see his goodness extended toward you in his time. He will not disappoint you. When He restores what you have lost it *will* be worth your effort.

While you're waiting on God, read the next chapter. It will make it a lot easier for you to stick with your decision to wait and believe.

13. Challenge the Thief

Before God restores your prosperity, you have to
have faith that He will restore it. Before you can have
faith, you must know what his word says about the
matter, because faith comes from hearing God's word.
So we will begin by taking a look at God's laws that
govern restitution, his legal process by which stolen
goods are returned to the victim.

You already know who the victim is, but you may
not realize that Satan, whom I referred to earlier as the
squatter, is also called *the thief*. Though God sent the
famine, it is Satan who, with God's permission, steals
what is yours. You opened the door to Satan to occupy
your property—which, like all tenants from Hell, he
always destroys—when you or your spouse knowingly
or unknowingly violated God's word. Satan deceived
you into thinking you can ignore God's word and
prosper. He deceived you into thinking that the
prosperity and success you enjoyed in the past were
largely of your own making and not the direct result of

93

God's blessing. He lulled you into thinking you could sow evil (by omission or commission) and not reap destruction. Deception is Satan's only weapon, but as all those who have suffered famine have learned, it is a deadly one. God's people are destroyed for lack of knowledge. (Hosea 4:6) For you, the destruction can end right now.

But, you say, it wasn't Satan at all! It was a customer who stole from you. Or your partner ran off with the payroll. Or your spouse sued you for everything you owned in common and left you penniless. Or you were fired or laid off or injured and couldn't work or some other tragedy came into your life to rob you. But these events are only tools God used to wake you up to his will. Satan is under God's thumb. He performs his evil assignment of stealing, killing, and destroying primarily through people. Because they walk in spiritual darkness in some area of their thinking, they believe the lies and act on the wicked promptings Satan whispers into their minds. Satan's playground is any area of a person's mind unenlightened by God's word. Galatians 2:2 says Satan works through those who are ignorant of or disobedient to God's word. (This is true of Christians and non-Christians alike. Even well-meaning Christians can be ignorant of God's truth in some way or another, which creates opportunity for them to be deceived by Satan, ultimately hurting themselves and other Christians in the process.)

So even though people have stolen from you, they are not your problem, Satan is. The Bible says we "wrestle not against flesh and blood (*people*) but against principalities, against powers, against the rulers of the darkness of this world, against spiritual wickedness in high places." (Ephesians 6:12) Because your battle with famine is spiritual, you must use spiritual weapons to win back the blessings you have lost.

Colossians 2:15 says Jesus defeated Satan, "spoiling principalities and powers," that is, Jesus completely divested Satan of his power (spoil, from Greek *apekduomai,* "to divest wholly"). God has given *you* authority over Satan. Jesus has given *you* power to trample on Satan and his cohorts, "Behold, I give unto you power to tread on serpents and scorpions (*demonic spirits*), and over all the power of the enemy." (Luke 10:19) Jesus has broken Satan's power off you and what is yours, "Who hath delivered us from the power of darkness, and hath translated us into the kingdom of his dear Son." (Colossians 1:13)

Now that you know who the real thief is that's been stealing from you, you need to know what God's law says about his punishment. Although God allowed Satan to rob you because of your or your spouse's sin— in the same way He allowed the Gentiles to afflict the Israelites because of the Israelites' sin—rest assured that He punishes those who harm his children. He destroyed the Gentiles for their wickedness, and He will rend from Satan's kingdom all he has stolen from you and more.

Here is a long Bible passage but it is critical to your restoration. You have to understand God's stance on restitution to have faith that He'll restore what Satan has stolen from you. Look past all the references to livestock and stacks of corn and see God's principle of restitution:

If a man shall steal an ox, or a sheep, and kill it, or sell it; he shall restore five oxen for an ox, and four sheep for a sheep.

If a thief be found breaking up (entering someone else's property), and be smitten that he die, there shall no blood be shed for him.

If the sun be risen upon him, there shall be blood shed for him; for he should make full restitution; if he have nothing, then he shall be sold for his theft.

If the theft be certainly found in his hand alive, whether it be ox, or ass, or sheep; he shall restore double.

If a man shall cause a field or vineyard to be eaten, and shall put in his beast, and shall feed in another man's field; of the best of his own field, and of the best of his own vineyard, shall he make restitution.

If a fire break out, and catch in thorns, so that the stacks of corn, or the standing corn, or the field, be consumed therewith; he that kindled the fire shall surely make restitution.

If a man shall deliver unto his neighbor money or stuff to keep, and it be stolen out of the man's house; if the thief be found, let him pay double.

If the thief be not found, then the master of the house shall be brought unto the judges, to see whether he have put his hand unto his neighbor's goods.

For all manner of trespass, whether it be for ox, for ass, for sheep, for raiment, or for any manner of lost thing, which another challengeth to be his, the cause of both parties shall come before the judges; and whom the judgest shall condemn, he shall pay double unto his neighbor. Exodus 22:1–9

This is Old Testament, sure, but God's heavenly law of restitution, his sense of right and wrong, his demand for justice does not change. Justice: It's why Jesus had to die for us. Satan owes you big time, at least double what he's stolen from you. He is the ruler of the kingdoms of this world, and all it takes is one word from God and Satan must release your blessings from his grip. But what will it take to move God to demand that Satan release what He has stolen from you?

Look carefully again at verse 9. Here God tells you how to bring Satan to court to get your goods back:

"For all manner of trespass, whether it be for ox, for ass, for sheep, for raiment, or for any manner of lost thing, which another challengeth to be his, the cause of both parties shall come before the judges; and whom the judgest shall condemn, he shall pay double unto his neighbor."

You are the aggrieved party. Satan has stolen from you. Will you come before the judge to challenge Satan's actions? Will you accuse him? "Judges" here is from *elohiym,* or Elohim. It means GOD. It is up to you to go before God in prayer and point the finger at the true thief behind your suffering and loss. Quit complaining to God about all the people whom Satan has used to bring famine into your life and name the real culprit. Recognize that you are fighting a spiritual battle; fight with spiritual tools. Be bold! Expect justice! Tell God you want the double return on all Satan has stolen and then believe God to fulfill his word. You are not asking for too much. You are not greedy. *You are asking God to fulfill his own law of restitution.* After all, if you only got back what you lost, you wouldn't be fully restored. Double restitution makes up for your pain, suffering, lost time, and lost interest on your investments. Besides, it is scriptural to expect interest on what's yours—God does. See the parable of the talents, Matthew 25.

Sound too good to be true? It isn't. But to strengthen your faith, let's take a look at the stories of others whom God has restored multifold.

14. What God Will Do

You may struggle with the biblical concept of restoration, especially double restoration, because it is new to you and because you feel undeserving. Well we're all undeserving, but Jesus saved us anyway. What He did on the cross for us is vastly more costly to Him, more valuable to us, and more lasting than a double return of any job, career, house, company, car, real estate, or whatever Satan has stolen from you. So you might as well quit thinking that a double return of your goods is too much to ask for. In the eternal picture, you're asking for nothing. It's just stuff. Don't let it become bigger in your mind than it really is.

Despite the inferior and temporary nature of stuff, God knows it must be returned to make you whole, and He is gracious to get it to you. When He decides to do so, his action will be marked by two features: speed and completeness. Speed, so that you can clearly see his hand in the matter and won't be tempted to credit your turnaround to natural forces; completeness, so that you cannot say that God is not just in his dealings.

From the very day the Israelites repented of failing to put God first, the Bible says God promised to bless their crops. (Haggai 2:19) Their famine ended in one day. Not only did He promise to bless them materially but He promised to make the glory of the new temple they were building greater than the original, to draw all nations into it, and to bring peace.

In II Kings 6 God restored the Samaritans to prosperity, also in one day, just as Elisha prophesied. The starving Samaritans had reached the point where they were eating their own children when three lepers decided they had no choice but to sneak into the enemy's camp to beg for food. When they arrived they found the camp abandoned and clothing, food, equipment, and livestock strewn everywhere. The booty was sold at the city gate that day, ending the famine.

Another famine that ended suddenly, the one that meant the most to me when I was suffering my own, was the story of the Shunammite woman in II Kings 8. I rejoiced as I read this story one day, because it was that day that God quickened this passage to me and told me to begin believing Him to do for me what He'd done for her. His simple message wasn't lost on me: I knew He was going to return my home to me just as He returned the Shunammite woman's. After a time of meditation in this story, I began to believe Him to do more, however, than just give me a new house. II Kings 8 says that God also restored to the Shunammite woman in one day her seven years of lost income from the land. The more I read this passage, the more my faith grew that God would restore to me my seven years of lost income due to unemployment. I was no longer content just to have an income again. I wanted an income big enough to make up for the seven years when I had none. I wanted to be restored the way the Shunammite woman had been restored.

The account in Ruth of how God restored Elimelech is an especially beautiful story of God's grace. Of course, the focus of the book is Ruth, but to make you understand how fully God plans to restore you, there is no more revealing story than this rich account of God's goodness to Elimelech.

While trying to escape the famine God had sent to Israel, Elimelech and his two grown sons died in Moab without fathering children. The tragedy is that Elimelech fled to Moab precisely because he worried that the famine would destroy his family. I told you in chapter six that famine is designed to bring death into every area of your life. This is exactly what happened to Elimelech. Death moved into his house and settled into every room. First it overthrew Elimelech. Then it attacked the spiritual welfare of his children by deceiving them into marrying heathen women, a direct violation of God's law and a sure way to cause a dynasty to turn from the faith. Then it took his son's lives. Finally it spread its rapacious fingers into all that Elimelech owned in Moab, leaving Naomi not just alone, but destitute. "How can one enter into a strong man's house, and spoil his goods," says Matthew 12:29, "except he first bind the strong man? and then he will spoil his house." When Elimelech let his faith become bound by unbelief, he opened the door to Satan to rob his house, and rob it he did. Elimelech lost everything.

I remember well the pain I felt when we too lost everything. The loss of our home and my years of unemployment hurt every area of our lives. The foreclosure destroyed our excellent credit rating and crippled our effort to borrow money at a low interest rate. It left us with no cash reserve for emergencies, yet emergencies came anyway, and so we were forced to borrow money at rates that crushed us. When we could make only minimum payments and had to borrow more to meet yet another emergency, our debts grew to an impossible amount, increasing our sense of hopelessness. It meant we would never again qualify for a low-interest or no-down mortgage, and the money we should have been saving for our children's education—they were getting closer to college age every day, another major source of stress for me— would have to be spent on a large down payment to secure a manageable monthly mortgage payment. The enormous hole in my résumé caused by unemployment also was a constant worry to me. What would I tell a potential employer? That I couldn't get full-time work for seven years because God had sent famine to our home? I could see the interviewer dialing Security.

And how would I convince my four children that they can stand on God's laws of prosperity when it was obvious their parents had done nothing but struggle to feed and clothe them for seven years? Our kids knew we were trying to find a home to buy and that we were failing. How could they not know? We searched unsuccessfully for a house all those years; it was a regular dinner conversation topic. For the last two years before God ended the nightmare by supplying a mortgage-free home, every night before bed my oldest son faithfully went to the closet in the family room and pulled out two cots. He set them up with blankets and pillows, one at one end of the family room for his little

sister, one at the other end for himself. Every morning
he just as faithfully folded the bedding, knocked down
the cots, and stowed everything back into the closet in
the corner of the room. He and his sister slept this way
because our rental house was too small for the six of us.
My son slept comfortably, but he was old enough to
realize that all his friends had their own rooms, or at
least they had real beds. I was so ashamed.

But I would tell them, "God is faithful. He's going
to get us out of here. God is going to give us a house."
How hollow my words sounded when for so long we
continued to live, cramped and broke, in that little
house. I had seen better days and knew God's will was
to bless his people, but two of our children were just
tots when we lived well in Birmingham. They didn't
remember prosperity. The other two had been born
during famine and knew only struggle, sleeping on cots
and answering to a landlord.

As if losing the house, equity, job, and good credit
rating were not enough, I began to nurse a quiet fear
that we, like Elimelech, would also lose our children to
unbelief. During all those trying years I told them God
would prosper his people if they tithed and gave
offerings, but we were doing both and scraping by. I
told them God would provide us our own house, but all
they knew was life in a rental. I assured my oldest
daughter, a straight-A student, that God would provide
for her college education, but in my heart I was quaking
because I hadn't earned in years, and so much equity
had been lost in the house that the power to provide for
our daughter's education was no longer in our hands. I
feared my daughter would miss her opportunity to
attend a good college because of her parents' spiritual

folly. We were broke, terribly in debt, the six of us living on one income in a rented house that grew shabbier every year. Every day threatened a new financial disaster because we never had enough money in the bank to meet an emergency. Satan took advantage of our many evil circumstances to abuse my mind with doubt and fear, tormenting me every day with bleak scenarios concerning my children's walk with God and their chances for a good education. Would our children, like Elimelech's, lose faith in God's promises and embrace the world's system because of our stupidity? The guilt I felt was overwhelming. My depression knew no depth. At times I was suicidal.

But Naomi felt worse, I'm sure, on the day she walked into Bethlehem-Judah and had to tell her neighbors and friends that her husband and sons were dead. At least I was spared so great a loss. But the day that Naomi took that step was a pivotal one for her, because it ended the famine on Elimelech's house. God had provided Ruth, her Moabite daughter-in-law, to accompany her, and when they returned to Israel Ruth worked in the fields as a gleaner, providing food for them both. Then God arranged Ruth's marriage to Boaz, a relative of Elimelech, who "redeemed" the two women and Naomi's land, providing well for them until they died. Ruth, who treated Naomi "better than seven sons," (Ruth 4:15), provided an heir to be raised up in the name of Elimelech, so that his name was not forgotten in Israel after all—even more evidence of God's grace toward his wandering son. Finally, and most marvelous, is that Elimelech's family came to have a place in the lineage of Jesus Christ through

Ruth, even though her very presence in the land of Israel was due to his disobedience. Think of it: In the midst of all the spiritual death brought on by Elimelech's unbelief and disobedience, God was still able to work history-changing life. Nothing stopped Him from restoring the house of Elimelech.

The prodigal son was also restored to sonhood in one day, and not only restored, but honored and feted as never before. Job was more than restored after his ordeal, for he received double what he lost. When David and the people repented for Saul's sin, God quickly began to bless their harvests again. No record exists in the Bible where God would not or could not swiftly and completely restore his people to prosperity after having dealt with their sin by famine. Even when David sinned horribly in adultery with Bathsheba and the wicked affair of Uriah's murder (II Samuel 11), which resulted in God allowing David's firstborn to die, nevertheless, once David acknowledged his sin, God soon afterward sent a wondrous child, Solomon, who grew into a man of wisdom and power like no Israelite king before or after him.

So what mess have you made that God will not turn around? You know He can do it. Are you convinced He *will?* What dream of yours has been stolen by Satan's deception? It's *all* deception, friend. The thought that life will never get better, that you'll never have anything, that you'll never succeed, these are all Satan's lies. It doesn't matter how much you've lost, how much you've suffered, how badly you've erred, how severe the famine. You may feel that your life is destroyed and your dreams long ago dead and buried, but God's resurrection power is unchanged.

What's more, He specializes in bringing things back from the dead. God is able, and just as important, God is willing to undo everything Satan has done to rob you.

For seven years I mourned the loss of my home. Stung with humiliation over the foreclosure and ashamed in front of my kids, I listened to Satan when he whispered in my ear, "You'll never own another home. Or if you do, the monthly payments will be so high that you'll have nothing to help your kids with college expenses." Those two thoughts caused me so much grief. *But they weren't true.*

Here's the truth. One day during the construction of our new home, I stood across the street from the lot, contemplating the fact that my family and I would soon be living in our own brand new, five-bedroom home just three blocks from our rental house. The house was half built, and I could never get enough of watching the workmen labor on my dream. As I stood there gazing on my miracle, God spoke two words into my spirit that forever changed my life.

"Satan lied."

I was stunned. Then I started to cry. *That's right!* I thought. *Every evil thing that I feared would come about because of famine was a lie!* The depressing future that Satan had whispered into my ears to discourage me never came to pass! God had a plan all along through those seven years of famine. He never meant to crush us, only to correct us. He used Satan to do it, but He was never going to let Satan win. God was always in control no matter how out of control things looked. The mental torture I had endured for so long was only because I had believed Satan's lies. How clear it all seemed at that moment.

We moved into our new home in August 1997. Since then our oldest daughter has finished college and graduate school, and at almost no expense to her parents, spent one year working and studying in Germany, a dream she had voiced since early high school. As I write this, her three siblings are following her into a college education.

It's time to close, and I've kept you waiting long enough. Now I'm going to tell you how God restored to me and my family everything Satan snatched away.

15. *What God Did for My Family*

Even though I know what needs to be said, I've procrastinated shamelessly in writing this final chapter. I fear you will focus on my blessing and not God's intervention, or that you will think it impossible or unlikely for God to replicate in your life the deliverance He worked for me because my circumstances were different than yours. Nothing could be further from the truth, of course, but the fact that you picked up this book indicates you're beaten down in some area of your life, likely your finances. Consequently it might be hard for you to believe to see God's goodness expressed in your situation to the same miraculous degree He worked for me. Nevertheless I hope you open the ears of your spirit and receive with faith my amazing story.

After fasting one day a week for months, there came a day—I'm not certain exactly when—that God spoke to me that I had fasted long enough. I believe it was late 1996 or early 1997 when I heard this word.

About this same time my widowed father became

engaged to a lovely woman he met at church. Because my three sisters and I were all grown by then, and because his impending marriage would force changes to his will, my father visited his attorney for advice concerning his estate. My father owned the house he lived in and two other homes, all mortgage free, and his plan was to leave a home to three of his daughters. The fourth would receive his savings account. But my father received advice that convinced him that his estate plan was lopsided. He needed to purchase a fourth home for cash and give it to one of his daughters before he died. If he failed to take this step, one daughter would be left the bulk of his estate in cash and would do just fine. The other three would inherit his homes, but they wouldn't have the means to pay inheritance (and in some cases, property) taxes on those properties.

So to distribute his estate equitably, my father bought me a home. I'm the only person I've ever known who received an inheritance before the death of the testator.

I can hear you say, "But my parents don't have money to help me." I understand that. My parents weren't rich either. My father was a mailman, my mother was a secretary. But that's not the point.

The point is that there is a deliverance from famine for whoever calls upon the Lord. No matter the method, deliverance is *God's doing*. You may be limited by your circumstances, but He is not. God saved the Samaritans from famine by the faith of three lepers, not a mighty army. The widow of Sarepta was delivered by offering just a handful of meal and a bit of oil, not a lottery ticket. If you have faith, even just a little bit of faith, nothing can stop you from being restored. Both the lepers and the widow were impoverished, but their acts of faith and obedience brought deliverance. Remember, it's not your need that moves the hand of God, it's your faith.

Further, God isn't looking to replicate your deliverance in the same way He did it for me, and odds are, He won't. Your circumstances are different—your deliverance will be different. But in this it will be the same: He will use natural channels—people—to bring about your deliverance. You will receive divine favor, unexpected blessings, from sources you never thought possible. God delights in using the weak things of the world to confound the wise, because He wants the glory for your deliverance to shine on Him and no other. And don't you think that your unique deliverance, different from anyone else's, brings Him more glory than a repeat performance?

Equally important: The problem with receiving a mortgage-free home is that the very idea of it is too big in our minds. We think God has done some phantasmagorical feat in providing a house without a mortgage. Yes, I got my miracle, and I certainly wouldn't trivialize that fact. But as I told you earlier, I had been believing for an affordable mortgage, nothing more. I didn't have the faith for a mortgage-free home. Actually, such a thing had never entered my mind. But I have to confess, as I stood across the street in the summer of 1997, watching the construction crew labor to finish our new, five-bedroom, three-and-a-half bath house, it struck me with the sizzling power of a lightning bolt that, my entire Christian life, I had undervalued the work of the cross. I say this because as I watched in utter awe as my miracle was being built right in front of me, it dawned on me that I had never transferred that same degree of awe to the work of salvation. Here I was, jumping up and down on a suburban street in northern Virginia, marveling at what God had done for me and my family. And it was just *stuff.* It was just earthly shelter (albeit very, very nice shelter). And it was temporary, unlike salvation, which is eternal.

The take-away from this revelation is that it is easy for God to restore to you what Satan has stolen. Compared to what He accomplished on the cross, getting your stuff back is a cinch. Above all, remember this: It was never MY idea to receive a mortgage-free home—*it was entirely God's idea.* Let that sink in. A house of wood and brick or eternal life with Jesus Christ, enjoying the glory and beauty of the wonders of his Heaven. Which is the bigger miracle? Which costs Him more? Which is of greater, lasting value? Before our seven years of famine, I would have concluded that if God gave us lots of nice stuff—house, car, job—all the material goodies we enjoy, then He must love us a lot. Receiving those things from God makes us feel loved. And of course I understood salvation, what I was saved from, the agonies of the cross and the horrors of eternal Hell and separation from God. Naturally I was grateful to be delivered from all that.

But before our seven years of suffering, I did not understand, not really, the essential goodness and generous nature of God. In the years before famine my concept of God was (I see now) limited: I saw his mercy toward creation as something He *had* to exercise. He had to send Jesus to the cross to save us from eternal Hell fire because his mercy compelled Him. To not show mercy would be to violate his nature. But after our seven years of suffering, when I saw how God more than restored us, I realized that God is not only merciful, He's good, truly good. He's gracious, and above all, He's generous. He didn't have to bless us to the extent that He did. He blessed us so abundantly because He *wanted* to.

Of course He's willing to give us wonderful things, material and spiritual, during our short tenure on earth. If He sent his Son to the cross and Hell for us, what will He not give us besides? A nice house to live in is nothing compared to our salvation. The house is not the goal. It's just icing on the cake, a daily reminder of his love.

Your circumstances are different than mine, so your restoration story will be different than mine. But it doesn't matter how God restores you. All that matters is that He wants to and He will. I've written my story so that you can read, believe, act, and see the hand of God deliver you from famine. I pray you do what you must do to secure your deliverance, today.

About the Author

Virginia (Ginny) Hull Welch was raised in Santa Clara, California, where she earned a Bachelor's in English. She married and moved to northern California where she earned a Master's in communications at California State University, Chico and where she was first paid for her writing: $25 for a two-page magazine article on how to get a permanent job through temporary work. Since those early days she has worked as a newspaper (foods and politics) writer, book editor, proposal writer and editor, and freelancer—moving around the United States as she followed her husband's job transfers. She has four grown children and now resides in Virginia. What to Do When the Blessings Stop – When God Sends Famine is her third book.

Www.ginnywelch.com